MW00680111

In this uniquely-styled, and very enjoyable book, Dr. Jackson provides important historical context while revealing the economic reasoning skills that will help people achieve success in their personal, business, and civic lives. I highly recommend this excellent book which is a fitting tribute to a remarkable teacher-of-teachers, Dr. Paul Ballantyne, one of the giants of economic education.

—Robert L. Clinton

President, Colorado Council for Economic Education

Congratulations, your book *Better Off* has filled an international gap that has existed in my life since 1959. As President of the Tempe Sister Cities Program and as past President of Sister Cities International, one thing is clear to me after reading your book: *Better Off* will be recommended reading for all of Tempe's future citizen diplomats, both young and old.

—Dick Neuheisel

President, Tempe Sister Cities

Dr. Jackson has a gift for bringing economics to life in a clear and conversational way. He provides a real service with this book, explaining the keys to economic success, and how we might lose our way if we forget these keys. He has seen much in his life that he brings to bear in this fine book, and it is a particularly important read for young people today.

—Nicholas Muller

Attorney at Law

I absolutely loved this book. Dr Jackson makes the principles of economics easy and actually enjoyable to learn. He then builds on that foundation to explain how the USA used those principles to become the greatest economy in the history of the world. Dr. Jackson goes on to show us how to apply those principles in our own lives, and inspires us by showing how to succeed by making other people better off. I cannot recommend this book enough.

—Jonathan Manske

author, Law of Attraction Coach

Dr. Jackson's new book, *Better Off*, is one of the best books I have read on economics and cultural transformation. The book is extremely readable, educational, and practical. This book is so good, I was reading sections of it out-loud to my fourteen year-old daughter. *Better Off* should be required reading in all high schools and universities and also required reading for every state and federal employee. *Better Off* is one book I highly endorse and recommend. Share it with as many people as you can!

—Rev. Daniel B. Gilbert, Ph.D.

Read *Better Off* . . . it's quite likely that you'll recapture your smile, re-write your bucket list, and close the book cover full of optimism. This book just might change your life!

—Jim Myers

What a treat to read *Better Off*. I found it logical,
practical, and just plain common sense.

—Ron Gascho

banker

Dr. Jackson's travels and interactions with foreign governments have
given him a unique perspective on why the United States and its
individuals have been able to prosper, when other countries and
their citizens have not. He guides us through difficult concepts
with a writing style that had me whispering to myself as I read, *Oh,
now I understand!* Dr. Jackson challenges each of us to make the
world a better place by asking, "What'cha Gonna Do with What'cha
Got?" After reading this book, I know that I'm Gonna Do More.

—John A. McCarty, PE, PWLF

Executive Director, Southeast Metro Stormwater Authority

Wow, what a great read! It gives us an appreciation for what "The American
Experiment" was all about. We were handed freedom to innovate, create,
and make everyone better off. He explains the concept of scarcity versus
abundance and how it is possible to live in abundance. He also reminds
us that goodness is something we need to incorporate into all we do.

—Chris Anderson

Lam-Wood Systems Inc., Owner/CEO

Better Off provides insight into how our world's economies work, and why. I'm not sure which facet I enjoyed reading about more—the economic theory, the explanations of historical "experiments," or Dr. Jackson's personal observations and participation in the economies of many countries around the world. The discussion on how culture intersects with economics is incredibly thought-provoking, and left me wanting to put these principles into action. These ideas could really put the United States back on a path to being the greatest economy in the world, and making everyone "better off."

—John Haas

Love the book! Jim Jackson has seen first-hand the effects of forced redistribution of wealth in his travels, both with Project CURE and as an economic consultant to third world countries. In *Better Off*, he takes us through a crash course in economics. He ends by urging us all to use our talents not just to increase our own net worth, but rather, to contribute to the world we live in. I heartily recommend this intriguing book from one of the most effective humanitarians of our time.

—Peggy Yujiri

President, Council on Parents

BETTER OFF

BETTER OFF

HOW AMERICA
GOT WEALTHY &
YOU CAN TOO!

DR. JAMES W. JACKSON

Better Off
Published by Winston-Crown Publishing House, LTD
P.O. Box 651
Evergreen Colorado, 80437 USA

ISBN 978-1-61137-009-6

Cover Design and Interior Art: Linda Wood, LW design & art, LLC
Photo of Dr. Jackson: Jimmy Dozer, Jimmy's Fashion Art Photography

Library of Congress Control Number 2016902189.

Printed in the United States of America
2016—First Edition

21 20 19 18 17 16 / 6 5 4 3 2 1

For information about a special discount for bulk purchases, please contact Winston-Crown Publishing House LTD at press@winstoncrown.com or by phone 1-303-674-9790.

To my friend and esteemed professor of economics
Dr. Paul Ballantyne

CONTENTS

PART 3: A NEW ECONOMIC PARADIGM

ACKNOWLEDGMENTS

Years ago I had the privilege of studying under Dr. Paul Ballantyne, my graduate-level economics professor at the University of Colorado. His experience teaching at Sumy State University in Ukraine and Leningrad State University in Pushkin, Russia, and my economic-consulting experience in Africa, Ecuador, Peru, Venezuela, and Brazil gave us a great deal to talk about even outside the classroom.

When I wrote *What'cha Gonna Do with What'cha Got?*, Dr. Ballantyne mentored me and proofread my material.

At the University of Colorado, Dr. Ballantyne served as chairman of the department of economics, dean of the College of Letters, Arts, and Sciences, as well as director of the Center for Economic Education. In all, he served the university for forty-four years.

When the Soviet Union collapsed in the early 1990s, I was working with Project C.U.R.E. in Ukraine and had the unique privilege of collaborating with Dr. Ballantyne to train Ukrainian government officials and medical leaders in free-enterprise concepts and market-system economics. It was an exhilarating experience to watch those new Ukrainian leaders work with their legislature to change the old Communist laws. Those changes even splashed over into the new economic structures of other countries in the old Soviet Federation.

Some years later, Dr. Ballantyne and I each signed contracts with Winston Crown Publishing House to coauthor a book on cultural economics. But sad to say, time was not in our favor. Dr. Ballantyne's retirement, the tragic loss of his precious wife, and a diagnosis of dementia left that dream unfulfilled. However, Dr. Ballantyne invited me to his office and presented to me his personal library of economics books, his lecture notes, and his class-syllabus collection. I treasure those gifts beyond measure.

Better Off: How America Got Wealthy and You Can Too was written in honor of my dear friend Paul Ballantyne. It is the desire of my heart that it will be an enduring tribute to his life, his work, and his love of free enterprise.

I would also like to acknowledge Jennifer Lonas for her fine editing and her enthusiastic spirit.

CULTURAL ECONOMICS

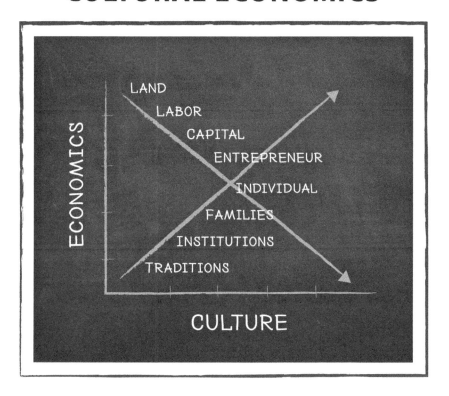

TRANSFORMATION
TAKES PLACE AT THE
INTERSECTION OF
CULTURE AND ECONOMICS

THE ROAD TO BETTER OFF

Nearly every election cycle, some politician raises the question, "Are you better off than you were four years ago?" For most Americans, "better off" has to do with economic prosperity.

- Am I earning more than I was four years ago?
- Can our family afford more "stuff," such as a bigger home or a nicer car?
- Can we afford to put the kids through college and save for retirement?

If we scan the economic landscape in the United States today, we see many families struggling just to pay the bills and put food on the table. Some are balancing precariously on the edge of financial disaster, with inflated consumer prices, suffocating taxation, and inadequate incomes threatening to push them over the edge into poverty. Others, seemingly immune to economic hardship, enjoy opulent lifestyles. Somewhere between these extremes, a record number of Americans are living quite comfortably off government benefits and handouts. But are they truly better off? What does *better off* really mean?

It's high time we answer that question, don't you think?

As a cultural economist, I've always had an insatiable curiosity about the way culture and economics intersect to bring about change. How does an economic system impact a culture, and conversely, how does a culture affect an economic system?

I find it curious, for example, that most Americans don't have a clue about the rapid economic and cultural changes we're experiencing or why they're happening.

They may sense intuitively that something is wrong, but they can't quite put a finger on the cause. They can't understand why there's such a big fuss over balanced budgets, debt limits, and deficit spending. Most important, they don't realize how cultural values and economic policies directly impact their ability to become better off. If they haven't learned the most basic economic concepts, how can they possibly understand what's happening or what they can do about it?

Trekking around this old world for more than thirty years as a businessman, consultant, and humanitarian has afforded me ample opportunities to observe the complex interplay between cultures and economic systems. Ultimately, what happens at the intersection of culture and economics determines the condition and direction of a country.

In my travels with Project C.U.R.E. (Commission on Urgent Relief and Equipment) to more than 150 countries, I witnessed firsthand the rise and fall of nations and political systems. I've studied the economic disparities and cultural flash points in countries like Rwanda that have ignited genocidal firestorms. I've marveled over politically bifurcated countries like Vietnam that have somehow overcome the ravages of war and become better off.

Cultural economics is an intriguing approach that not only enables us to understand the world but helps us figure out how and why transformation takes place. When I was a kid, my grandfather used to tell me, "Jimmy, if you want to know why something happens, follow the money." That's certainly true, but I've also discovered that if you really want to understand why and how things change, you must follow the money trail to the intersection where culture and economics meet head-on.

Traditional economists spend their time collecting economic data and producing charts, or matrices, to predict future conditions. But cultural economics is all about people. It explores how members of a society, with their particular behavior patterns, motives, beliefs, traditions, values, needs, abilities, and emotions, interact with and influence economic events and outcomes. Religious beliefs, for example, can influence the purchasing patterns of both individuals and groups. If you decide to export your successful Texas beefsteak chophouse franchise to Calcutta, India, don't expect to make a lot of money. In Texas, cows are wholesome, but in Calcutta, they're holy.

Anytime cultural and economic factors come together, we can count on change. Or as I like to say, *transformation takes place at the intersection of culture and economics*. I predict that change is here to stay … unless something changes. And in a world that's continually changing, cultural economics offers valuable insights into how we can become better off globally, nationally, corporately, domestically (as families), and individually. I personally like living in an ever-changing world because it's the only imaginable environment where we can all become better off.

After decades of observing and researching economic systems the world over, I've reached the conclusion that we are at a critical juncture in our nation's history; we desperately need to understand how the American experiment of 1776 made it possible for us to become one of the greatest and most prosperous nations in human history. And why preserving freedom—economically, politically, religiously, culturally, and individually—is essential to becoming better off once again. That is my vision for this book.

In the following chapters, we'll not only examine the great American experiment and its origins, but we'll identify some key factors that explain why some nations are poor and others are wealthy. In addition, we'll learn about the basic economic concepts that impact our everyday lives. As we do, we'll take dry economic theories off the library shelf and apply them in the marketplace, where real life happens.

On our journey, we'll discover how culture and economics intersect to bring about transformation in our world. We'll walk through history and observe the outcomes of cultural and economic experiments designed to make people better off. Finally, we'll explore the internal economic system that guides our choices and the role virtue can play in restoring the American dream and making us all better off.

Recently, a young lady told me that she lives by a simple motto: *go with what-ever is free and opt out of participating in the consequences.* That's her answer to be-coming better off.

Whatever motto you live by, I hope you'll join me on this adventure of discover-ing what *better off* really means. By the end of our journey together, I won't be at all surprised if you have a life-altering transformation of your own. Whether you realize it or not, you are an agent of change, and as a result of your own discoveries on this journey, you might just find yourself helping someone else become better off.

THE TRILLION-DOLLAR QUESTION

In more than three decades of international travel, I've had the opportunity to study hundreds of cultures and economic systems around the world, from wealthy countries basking in abundant peace, prosperity, and health to impoverished nations crippled by war, poverty, and disease.

The more I've observed the economic disparities between countries, the more my insatiable curiosity has worked overtime. Why are some countries wealthy while others are mired in poverty? Now that's a veritable trillion-dollar question.

Here are several others:

- Are the people in wealthy countries smarter than the people in developing countries? Do they have more advantages?
- Do people living in poverty lack the motivation to become better off? Are they just lazy?
- Do impoverished countries simply lack stable currencies?
- Why are many countries with abundant mineral deposits, fertile land, and a good climate locked in abject poverty?
- Do governments prefer a dependent citizenry so they're easier to control?

There are no easy answers to these and many other complex questions regarding the economic disparities between wealthy and impoverished nations, but I've observed some distinct patterns over the years that offer important clues regarding the root causes of poverty and the conditions necessary for prosperity.

Let's investigate these patterns and see what they tell us.

The Fruits of My Musings

In most poor and underdeveloped countries, I've observed an all-too-common pattern:

- Top-down control is enforced.
- Individual rights, freedoms, and initiative are minimized.
- Trade, business, and aspects of private life are increasingly regulated.
- Redistributive policies transfer wealth from one group of people to another as government leaders dictate.

When the state controls nearly every institution and economic activity, the people become stuck in a cycle of poverty and dependence. In time a country becomes impoverished as well.

In nearly every developing country in which I've worked, I've also noticed that leaders promised the people free medical care to gain their support and loyalty, but this eventually meant no medical care for anyone. It was a promise no leader could keep.

When people are sick, unable to work, and dependent on the government for support, it's impossible to build a strong economy. Healthy economies require healthy people. That's one of the reasons I founded Project C.U.R.E. in 1987. Since its inception, Project C.U.R.E. has donated well over a billion dollars' worth of medical supplies and equipment to hospitals and clinics around the world. We are also fully committed to fostering accountability and self-sufficiency in the countries where we work.

Hospitals receiving our medical goods give us prime opportunities to introduce the ideas of free market. For example, if they received an ultrasound or an x-ray machine we encourage them to begin charging the patient some amount for the service or goods. The amount need not be much and payment can even be made with duck eggs, chickens, a goat, labor at the hospital, or currency. But they need to learn that it is not free. The hospital can take the items to the market, sell the items and end up with discretionary income to purchase suture or bandages when we are not around. The results are spectacular.

Yet even with improvements in health care, the iron grip of poverty on a nation or an individual is almost impossible to break. If we were just dealing with a sterile set of economic graphs, charts, and matrices, we could pretty easily come up with a formula to eradicate poverty. Such a formula is what economists refer to as a *normative economic model*, which describes *what ought to be*. But the economic picture quickly gets murky when other variables come into play, including human nature in all its complexity and the tendency of power to lead to corruption and increased control. Adding to the confusion are ancient institutions and traditions that define beliefs and direct behaviors not only culturally but individually.

Throughout history, for instance, insecure people have turned to government to protect and take care of them from cradle to grave. Those in leadership wield *legitimate* authority and the power to *compel* obedience from the same people who empowered them. We tend to forget that each enacted law or regulation can ultimately be enforced with a gun! And leaders with unlimited power will do practically anything to retain that power. Human desires for security and power are just two of the variables that can complicate the economic picture.

Solving the problems that keep nations and individuals bogged down in poverty requires radical transformation. But destructive patterns are often deeply entrenched. It's extremely difficult to change traditions, institutions, family structures, and individual thinking about basic economic concepts like land, labor, capital, and entrepreneurship. (We'll explore these concepts later in the book). But unless this happens, the deadly cycle of poverty and oppression will continue.

By contrast, the dominant pattern I've observed among wealthy nations includes

- limiting centralized power through checks and balances;
- protecting and encouraging individual rights, freedoms, and initiative;

- promoting free enterprise;
- keeping taxes, restrictions on personal wealth, and regulations
  on trade and business to a minimum; and
- respecting the right to own private property.

Where freedom and limits on government are honored, individuals tend to flourish and become better off—and so does a country.

I find it alarming, however, that wealthy nations are turning away from the sound economic principles and policies that made them better off and are implementing unwise political and economic ideologies that have had an abysmal track record throughout history. As the old adage goes, "If it ain't broke, don't fix it." Yet that seems to be precisely what is happening today.

The reasons why some countries are mired in poverty while others enjoy abundant wealth are complex, but let's see if we can glean some clues from a couple of real-life examples.

A Tale of Two Countries

In the early 1980s, I embarked on one of my first international economic assignments in Zimbabwe, Africa. I was there at the invitation of prime minister Robert Mugabe—who later became president—and members of his cabinet. It didn't take long to realize that Zimbabwe wasn't the place for me. Civil war had not only claimed thousands of lives, but the government had also imposed a policy of forced redistribution of assets and property. However, I was there long enough to become well acquainted with the political and economic situation.

Formerly known as Rhodesia, the "bread basket of Africa," Zimbabwe has a population of more than thirteen million people and boasts some of the richest farmland on the face of the earth. The country also has one of the finest railroad systems in all of Africa, as well as the world's largest platinum reserves. In the past century, the Marange diamond fields were one of the greatest discoveries, but Zimbabwe is most famous for the great Zambezi River that flows over the majestic Victoria Falls.

Zimbabwe has everything imaginable to qualify it as one of the wealthiest countries in the world. But today it wallows in poverty. According to the Mundi index of gross domestic product (GDP), as of January 1, 2014, the per-capita earnings of the people of Zimbabwe amounted to just $600 per year. That's $1.64 per day. Out of 228 countries, Zimbabwe ranks 227.[1] Why?

Next, let's consider a little spot on the globe called Hong Kong. More than seven million people inhabit this 400-plus-square-mile parcel of land bordering the South China Sea. Most residents emigrated to Hong Kong from Guangdong Province in China to escape conflict. In 1997, Great Britain returned Hong Kong to the People's Republic of China, and it has remained under Chinese rule ever since.

Hong Kong possesses very little arable land and almost no natural resources, except for a shoreline sufficient for a port. As of 2013, the Hong Kong dollar was the thirteenth most traded currency in the world.[2] The tiny administrative region has become one of the most important financial centers in the world, following New York and London,[3] and is considered the epicenter for management, finance, Internet technology (IT), business consultation, and professional services.

Hong Kong has a well-developed transportation system and is lauded for the exquisite quality of life its residents enjoy. In fact, life expectancy in Hong Kong is one of the highest in the world—eighty years for men and eighty-five for women.[4]

Year after year, the Heritage Foundation's Index of Economic Freedom has listed Hong Kong as the freest market economy in the world.[5] The Mundi index of per-capita income ranks Hong Kong sixteenth in the world, with individual earnings at nearly $53,000 per year.[6] That's $145 per day, or approximately 90 times more than the folks in Zimbabwe earn in a year.

Hong Kong doesn't possess even a fraction of the natural and human resources available to Zimbabwe, and yet it's one of the wealthiest regions on earth. Why?

The hunt for clues continues.

2

★ ★ ★

THE ORIGINS OF BETTER OFF

In our quest to understand why some nations are wealthy and others are poor, we've examined some observable patterns that characterize each of them and considered two real-life examples. Now let's explore the origins of better off, which can be traced back to the greatest civilizations in human history and the ingenious cultural-economic experiments that transformed the world.

Alexander's Experiment

In 336 BC, a youth in his early twenties ascended to the Macedonian throne following the assassination of his father, King Philip II. Alexander was previously schooled at the feet of the Greek philosopher Aristotle, who made Alexander aware of an economically fragmented world divided into countless little city-states. Each dominion had its own government and legal system, military, currency, language, religions, and customs. But the costs of fragmentation were enormous: suffocating taxation, rampant poverty, and widespread "barriers to communication and commerce that had lain over Europe, the Mediterranean, and Asia Minor like a spiderweb."[1] With Aristotle's help, Alexander began to comprehend the destructive impact of fragmented economies.

In the ensuing years, Alexander the Great conquered the known world and introduced sweeping economic reforms, establishing unity, security, fairness, a common currency, and low taxes throughout his empire. He also encouraged free trade based on a dependable coinage of gold and silver. The genius of Alexander's economic experiment lay in the fact that those benefits cost his constituents a whole lot *less* rather than a whole lot more. Previously his citizens had been paying exorbitant taxes to support their fragmented city-states, but Alexander made drastic reductions in their tax rates. Little wonder that many cities threw open their gates and welcomed the Macedonian conqueror with open arms.[2]

Alas, by 323 BC, the young ruler died of a high fever at the age of thirty-three following a wild drinking party. After his untimely death, his obtuse and greedy generals torpedoed the experiment and divided up the empire. Consequently, Alexander's empire began to crumble, but his dream and his legacy lived on. He had brought greater unity and stability to Europe, established peace through religious dominance, fostered commerce and trade in the Mediterranean, and spread Greek culture, literature, philosophy, and art throughout Asia Minor.[3] Although Alexander's Macedonian Empire faded into history, his reforms transformed the world and paved the way for future prosperity.

A Roman Makeover

Centuries later, Julius Caesar resurrected Alexander's dream in another great experiment that eventually became known as the Pax Romana. The global economy Caesar inherited wasn't quite as fragmented economically as it had been prior to Alexander's reign, however. Greek philosophy and literature, as well as elemental democracy, had largely succeeded in breaking down barriers between the Greeks and the barbarians. Like Alexander, Caesar built his empire through economic and political liberation.[4]

After conquering Gaul, Caesar invaded Italy, crossing the Rubicon in 49 BC. The citizens of Rome threw open their gates for their new leader and gave him a hero's welcome.[5] Caesar made the stability of Roman currency so attractive, the low taxation so alluring, and the opportunities for world trade and commerce so desirable that his empire expanded by the force of demand. He treated conquered nations so benevolently that even if they could have revolted, they didn't.[6]

Caesar accurately perceived that rewarding individual initiative and creativity would produce even *more* individual initiative and creativity, which would ultimately lead to a more stable and wealthy empire. By contrast, excessive taxation would squelch initiative and creativity. So Caesar wisely established an economic system that would not only benefit his empire but would also make his citizens better off.

Many of Caesar's economic policies benefited the poor, including land distribution and building programs. He also established bankruptcy laws, scaled back exorbitant interest rates and debt, eliminated provincial tax collection, and fortified the currency by backing it up with gold.[7]

As the impact of Caesar's ingenious experiment spread throughout the world, trade flourished and the economy expanded. In spite of its corruption and eventual demise, the Roman Empire was unquestionably one of the greatest civilizations in human history, and many who lived under its shadow became better off.

The Pax Britannica

In spite of its colonialistic fervor, the British Empire is a marvelous example of how global transformation takes place at the intersection of culture and economics.

By the nineteenth century, the military, political, and economic dominance of Great Britain had ushered in a period of peace and prosperity that would eventually be referred to as the Pax Britannica. Like the empires of Alexander the Great and Rome, the cultural and economic systems Great Britain implemented during this pivotal epoch in history helped to make the world better off.

The most pronounced and accelerated economic development in Great Britain took place between 1815 and 1850. By 1870, this comparatively small country was producing half the world's coal supply, and its exports surpassed the combined totals of Germany, France, and Italy. It also outpaced the United States in exports by three to one. Between 1830 and 1873, the production of pig iron—a crude form of iron converted to steel or wrought iron—skyrocketed from a mere 700,000 tons to approximately 6.5 million tons per year. The cotton industry was the primary driving force in the economy, and by 1841, more than 10 percent of workers were employed in textile mills.[8]

It has been said that the Industrial Revolution began in Great Britain.[9] And considering the exponential growth and innovation that occurred in practically every sector of the economy, along with the nation's military and political prowess, it's not surprising that Britain rose to world dominance.

Had it not been for the Magna Carta, however, the Pax Britannica might never have come about. Often dubbed the "Great Charter of Freedom," the Magna Carta of 1215 restricted the power of England's king, granted specific property and inheritance rights to the nobility, and even guaranteed legal protections for common citizens. Consequently, King John and his successors to the throne were required to abide by the rule of law and grant their subjects habeas corpus, or the right to request legal justification for detention, arrest, or imprisonment.

Such a document might not have been necessary if King John hadn't been such a tyrant—but it's a good thing for us that he was. When forty of his barons had had enough of his bullying, they presented their demands to the king in the Magna Carta. Forthwith, the king was informed that he would face a bloody civil war if he refused to ratify it.

Confronted with the specter of war, King John took out his royal feather pen and signed on the dotted line. Those forty barons who penned the Magna Carta couldn't have imagined the impact this document would have on a future nation that would be grounded in liberty and forged upon the truth that "all [people] are created equal [and] are endowed by their Creator with certain unalienable rights."[10]

This extraordinary charter wasn't finalized until 1225, but the rights, protections, and freedoms it guaranteed ultimately inspired the American experiment of 1776 and paved the way for the Declaration of Independence, the US Constitution, and the Bill of Rights. The roots of that experiment run straight from Runnymede, England, where the Magna Carta was signed, to Independence Hall in Philadelphia, Pennsylvania, where a free and independent nation was born.

Now that we've traced the historical roots of better off, let's turn our attention to the greatest cultural-economic experiment the world has ever known.

AN IMPROBABLE
EXPERIMENT

In 1776, culture and economics collided head-on to bring about transformation on a scale the world had never seen before—and perhaps will never see again. No other setting could have spawned an experiment like the one that took place across the Atlantic Ocean in the New World.

More than five hundred years earlier, the seeds of that experiment were planted in Runnymede, England, with the signing of the Magna Carta. Those seeds eventually sprang to life on the rugged shores of America and burst into full bloom on July 4, 1776, at Independence Hall in Philadelphia, where fifty-six freedom-thirsty men staked their claim to liberty that day as they etched their names on parchment and declared the independence of the thirteen "united states" of America.

The colonists who settled in America came from England or other parts of Europe. So why didn't they simply adopt the traditions, institutions, and systems of government from their homelands and get on with business in the New World? The answer is simple: the old systems and institutions proved to be inadequate as business models for this new American experiment. Colonization was a model for establishing new trade routes, new markets, and new revenues for greater prosperity throughout the British Empire. But it failed to allow for the equal participation of all citizens. America was destined to forge a bold new model for business and government.

As we'll see in this chapter, the Revolutionary War wasn't merely a clash over tea and taxes between an unruly bunch of American colonists and an oppressive British monarchy. It was an epic slugfest over economic and philosophical ideals about the rule of law, property rights, personal liberty, and representative government. Those ideals had been brewing in the hearts and minds of the revolutionary dreamers for a long time.

Had the war been merely a colonial power grab, the victorious revolutionaries would have established a new government that resembled the old one and crowned George Washington king of the colonies. Valuable property would have been divided into royal real estate, and prominent leaders would have been granted titles of nobility.

But English common law was the game changer. The majority of colonial revolutionaries were familiar with the concepts of common law, and they were determined not to allow some willy-nilly government of the day to set the rules for the New World. In fact, they were willing to stake their very "Lives, … Fortunes and … sacred Honor" on it.[1]

Patrick Henry, one of the most colorful orators in the fight for liberty, declared,

> We have done everything that could be done to avert the storm which is now coming on. We have petitioned—we have remonstrated—we have supplicated—we have prostrated ourselves before the throne, and have implored its interposition to arrest the tyrannical hands of the ministry and Parliament. Our petitions have been slighted; our remonstrances have produced additional violence and insult; our supplications have been disregarded; and we have been spurned, with contempt, from the foot of the throne.
>
> In vain … may we indulge the fond hope of peace and reconciliation. *There is no longer any room for hope.* If we wish to be free—if we mean to preserve inviolate those inestimable privileges for which we have been so long contending—if we mean not basely to abandon the noble struggle in which we have been so long engaged, and which we have pledged ourselves never

to abandon until the glorious object of our contest shall be obtained—we must fight! … Three millions of people, armed in the holy cause of liberty, and in such a country as that which we possess, are invincible by any force which our enemy can send against us. … We shall not fight our battles alone. There is a just God who presides over the destinies of nations, and who will raise up friends to fight our battles for us. …

The war is inevitable—and let it come! I repeat it, sir, let it come! … Is life so dear, or peace so sweet, as to be purchased at the price of chains and slavery? Forbid it, Almighty God! I know not what course others may take; but as for me, give me liberty, or give me death![2]

The colonies had endured such "a long train of abuses and usurpations" at the hand of King George III that they finally reached their limit. It was time "to dissolve the political bands" that had shackled them to the British monarchy and "Assume … the separate and equal station to which the Laws of Nature and of Nature's God [entitled] them."[3]

The men who gathered at Independence Hall to craft the Declaration of Independence knew that the document must be written with great skill and care, so they assigned the task to a gifted statesman by the name of Thomas Jefferson. Jefferson embraced the task wholeheartedly and set forth to compose one of the most eloquent founding documents in history. On behalf of the colonies, he declared that in the face of "absolute Despotism," they had no alternative but to rise up against the king of England. Indeed, Jefferson wrote, "It is their right, it is their duty, to throw off such Government, and to provide new Guards for their future security."[4]

The men who signed the Declaration of Independence were deadly serious about throwing off the tyranny of Britain. They rightly perceived that their signatures on such a document would be considered an act of treason punishable by hanging, but they were willing to pay the ultimate price for freedom. Although none of the signers was hanged for treason, many reportedly suffered great physical and financial hardships as a consequence of their actions:

- Francis Lewis's home was burned, and his wife was thrown in prison for several months. Her health was already fragile before the ordeal, and she died two years later.[5]
- The British destroyed John Hart's farm and hunted him like an animal for months. He died during "the gloomiest period" of the revolution in 1780, deprived of witnessing the victory of independence he sacrificed so much to attain.[6]
- After saving his family from the British, Richard Stockton was captured and treated with "great severity" as one of the signers of the Declaration. The British destroyed his estate, and he suffered greatly in prison from cold and hunger. He died in 1781 at the age of fifty-one.[7]
- Arthur Middleton lost most of his estate when the British invaded South Carolina, and he was imprisoned for nearly a year after the fall of Charleston.[8]
- After signing the declaration, William Hooper and his family endured continual harassment from the British, who threatened their lives and destroyed their property.[9]
- Thomas Nelson Jr. made great personal and financial sacrifices to support the war effort, and according to some accounts, when the British occupied his luxurious mansion, he "did not hesitate to bombard it."[10]

John Adams later remarked, "You will never know how much it cost the present Generation to preserve your Freedom! I hope you will make good use of it."[11]

Many of these men paid dearly to secure freedom for future generations of Americans and to forge a new system of government in which individual rights and the rule of law would be its very heart and soul. The American revolutionaries viewed the law not as an instrument of state control or manipulation but as a way for any individual citizen to seek redress of grievances. Based on a much higher and nobler concept than previously envisioned, the rule of law called for an independent body to craft a constitution that would become a beacon of freedom and hope for the nation and the world. That's precisely what America's new leaders set about doing as soon as the dust settled on the battlefield and the British sailed for home, defeated both militarily and philosophically.

Uncommon Denominators

The ideals of the American experiment of 1776 were like a breath of fresh air in a freedom-starved world. An unwavering system of checks and balances would rein in the executive, legislative, and judicial branches of government, and no leader would be considered above the law. Lawmakers would be directly accountable to voters through the ballot box, and the people would have a say in matters that directly affected them. In addition, no taxes would be levied or laws passed without the consent of the governed.

Citizens would be free from knee-jerk justice, and their property would be protected from being confiscated on a whim. Property rights would be absolutely secure, and disagreements would be arbitrated by magistrates.

Furthermore, a national constitution would guarantee God-ordained, individual rights, including the freedom of assembly, the freedom of speech, and the freedom of religion. The new government would not only protect these individual rights but would seek to "establish Justice, insure domestic Tranquility, provide for the common defence, promote the general Welfare, and secure the Blessings of Liberty."[12]

The 1776 experiment seemed to find a perfect niche in history, but it was an anomaly at the time—and it still is.

Over a lifetime of working in developing countries, I've observed that leaders with strong personalities typically grab positions of power and impose rules that promote their own selfish interests. Nepotism, advantages gained through status and ethnicity, the use of the military to consolidate power, the elimination of one's opponents, and the systematic looting of natural and human resources are just a few of the common denominators I've noted among newly established systems of government.

The American experiment, however, was characterized by a number of *uncommon* denominators:

- No entrenched economic or cultural system had to be eliminated or purged following the Revolutionary War. When the British were defeated, they simply went home.
- Many colonists were already familiar with the writings of John Locke and Adam Smith.
- The founders agreed that the newly formed government should answer to the people. It was to be a nation established "by the people [and] for the people."[13]
- The English Magna Carta became the model for the American Bill of Rights.
- British common law, which included property rights, formed the backdrop for the framers of the US Constitution.
- The people agreed on the concepts of elected leaders, term limits, and a peaceful transfer of power.
- The colonies had no monarchical social caste system of inherited titles and properties.
- Colonists were open to changes in the system.
- No aggressive neighboring countries were poised to attack the fledgling nation and steal choice land or seaports.
- The colonies had no oppressive demands from a state church to contend with.
- Colonists had a strong work ethic, which helped them survive harsh conditions. The land was rough, but the people were tough.
- The New World offered plenty of space to grow and welcome new legal immigrants.
- Colonists were moral, God-fearing people who were honest and industrious.

- The American people had the advantage of speaking a common language (English).
- The Atlantic Ocean provided a natural buffer between England and America.
- Colonists were forced to become independent from their homelands but reliant on their fellow citizens in the New World.
- The people expected dignity and equal opportunity rather than equal outcomes.

These unique factors set the stage for the great American experiment and the blessings of prosperity that would follow. When the curtain finally lifted and the drama began, the nation that emerged from the bloody revolution blazed with the unquenchable fire of liberty in her soul and beckoned the world to follow.

"The Last Best Hope of Earth"

The more I study the improbable experiment of 1776, the more I marvel that the framers were able to get it off the ground, much less articulate the ideals embodied in our founding documents. But fly it did.

Transformation takes place at the intersection of culture and economics, and the American experiment was no exception. It rocked the very foundations of the oldest institutions known to humankind and ushered in an era of achievement, creativity, and productivity that soared beyond the founders' wildest dreams.

But this improbable experiment was never guaranteed to continue in perpetuity. No insurance policy could protect it from tainted human nature, flawed systems, or corrupt institutions. Freedom is truly just "one generation away from extinction," as Ronald Reagan once said. Whether the great American experiment will endure in any recognizable form in the future, I cannot say. But in the pages of this book, we can find the road map to restoring and preserving the dream so that future generations will have the opportunity to become better off.

People often ask whether the experiment of 1776 reflects the system we have in America today. The simple answer is no. Yet in spite of all the attempts to trans-form our system into some replica of European socialism, I'm convinced that Abra-ham Lincoln had it right: America is still the "last best hope of earth." Even now, that improbable experiment of 1776 lives on and offers us and those who follow in our footsteps the opportunity to become better off.

PART **1**

A CRASH
COURSE IN
ECONOMICS

4

THE BASICS

I commented earlier that our economy and culture are going through incredibly rapid changes in the twenty-first century, but most Americans are clueless about what these changes mean or why they're happening. At the root of this ignorance is often a simple lack of knowledge.

To understand these changes and pinpoint the causes, we need a basic knowledge of economic concepts. And unless we grasp these concepts, we can't comprehend how and why our economic system works. We also can't fully appreciate the genius of the American experiment and how it created an atmosphere of unprecedented human achievement, creativity, and productivity that gave people the opportunity to become better off.

In the following chapters, we'll learn about change and scarcity, the money supply, the banking system, the Federal Reserve, inflation, and monetizing the federal debt. But before we dive into the deep end of the pool, let's start off with a very practical illustration that will bring economics out of the clouds into everyday life.

Cradle Economics

Most of us aren't quite as clueless about economics as we may think we are. We were born with some innate economic smarts that came in quite handy when we were kids. By the time we were six or seven years old, we were actually very proficient junior economists.

Economics—derived from the Greek word *oikos* ("a house") and *nemein* ("to manage")—simply deals with why and how people produce, distribute, and consume goods and services. By extension, an *economy* or economic system represents the way goods and services are organized and managed.

As children, we learn basic economics as we begin to communicate what we have to *produce*, what we want to *consume*, when we want to consume it, and under what conditions we're willing to *trade*. An infant easily grasps the concept of *supply and demand* in the nursery. He needs food, and his mother is able and willing to supply that demand. He comprehends from the start that this *transaction* requires at least two people: a demander (*consumer*) and a supplier (*producer*).

The demander and supplier designations work both ways simultaneously. Junior is not just a demander; he is also a supplier. He demands to be fed, but he can also supply peace and quiet. Mom supplies the food, but she can also demand peace and quiet. The *terms of the trade* must be negotiated and agreed upon, and in this case, the terms are *food* in exchange for *peace and quiet*.

Oh, but soon Junior learns he has other *marketable products*, such as love and affection. A big, gummy smile and cooing sounds are highly marketable *commodities*. Reaching out his chubby, little arms and hands and happily letting other people cuddle him are also very desirable. So he expands his *marketplace* of favors and discovers he can increase the appreciation level for his peace-and-quiet commodity by perfecting a *counterbalancing product* of crying and screaming.

Eventually Junior learns that if he wants something from another person, he must *trade* something in return. Those two somethings must be roughly of *equal value*, because in a *voluntary exchange*, everyone in the deal must end up *better off*.

A smelly deal teaches Junior that *price is a ratio of product values* and not just a single number. He has a dirty diaper that needs to be changed, but where's Mom? Alas, she's in the kitchen having coffee with her friend. And suddenly Junior is introduced to *competition*.

It's not that Mom is unwilling to change the diaper, but the terms of the trade must be established, and the price must be negotiated. Junior makes his demands known and builds in a real appreciation for his supply of peace and quiet. By trial and error, he discovers that two whimpers, four cries, and two screams equal one clean diaper (*price as a ratio of product values*).

As Junior grows, he discovers a new level of economic negotiations: "Son, if you'll clean up your bedroom, I'll let you stay up and play one more video game."

This requires the lad to *manufacture a product* before he can bring it to the marketplace for a trade. He has to *invest* in producing a product (a clean room) based on his mother's *promise* to let him stay up. He just discovered *credit*—the promise to pay upon receipt of the goods.

Now the boy decides to test the *stability of the monetary system*: "Okay, Mom, I'm ready for you to inspect my room."

"Son! Your clothes aren't picked up, and your bed isn't made. But that's okay, honey, You did pretty well. You can still stay up and play your game."

The *monetary standard* has just declined. The system has experienced *inflation*, because it will cost Mom more than the amount of the old reward to get the room cleaned properly next time.

Or Junior may clean his room properly and elect to use his mom's *credit promise* as *money*, exchanging it for something he would rather have in the future. That option is called *capital investment*, in which the boy gives up *current consumption* in anticipation of *future consumption*.

From our earliest days, we learn that *supply always equals demand*, even if a trade is never consummated, since each partner may just demand (or decide to keep) his own supply rather than trade for the other partner's supply. When a trade fails, each partner keeps his own supply, and yet supply still equals demand.

Isn't this fun? I bet you didn't know all of this was economics.

A Whirlwind Tour of Economic Systems

In a nutshell, a functioning economy must produce goods and services to generate income. Income can only be created when natural and human resources are used efficiently to produce desired goods and services. In turn, goods and services can be used to meet the internal needs and requirements of a country, or they can be traded in the world market to meet the needs of other countries (i.e., exports). When an economic system is functioning successfully, everyone has the opportunity to become better off.

Here's a little scenario that will help you better understand how our economic system works:

Meet Eddie Entrepreneur. Eddie is a hot-dog vendor—a **PRODUCER**.

The hot dog Eddie plans to sell is called a **PRODUCT**.

It is comprised of a bun, a wiener, ketchup, relish, and mustard. These are **RAW MATERIALS**. Eddie puts all these raw materials together to make the product.

Polly Purchaser is a hungry customer—a **CONSUMER**—who wants to buy one of Eddie's hot dogs.

If Eddie allows Polly to buy a hot dog, the *transaction* is called a **SALE**. The amount Polly pays for the hot dog is called the **PRICE**.

The *instrument* Polly uses to pay for the hot dog is *money*. Because Polly is willing to pay the price Eddie is asking, they have established a **MARKET VALUE.**

If no one else is selling hot dogs, Eddie has a *monopoly*. If other people are selling hot dogs, Eddie has **COMPETITION.**

Eddie's hot-dog stand is an *enterprise*, and the cost of getting into business is called **CAPITAL INVESTMENT.** What Eddie spends to operate his business and create his hot dogs is the *cost*.

Eddie has a plan to manage his capital investment. That plan is called a *budget*. If Eddies spends more than he budgeted, he creates a *budget deficit*. Whatever Eddie borrows to cover his deficit, including any other money he owes that he can't cover, is his **DEBT.**

The amount Eddie brings in from the sale of his hot dogs is called **INCOME.** If Eddie's income is *greater than* his cost, the difference is his **PROFIT.** If Eddie's income is *less than* his cost, the difference is a **LOSS.**

When the hot-dog business goes really well, Eddie sells lots of hot dogs. This is a *boom*. If his business activity slows down, he experiences a *recession or bust*.

If there is a sustained increase in all prices across the economy, including Eddie's hot dogs, it's called **INFLATION**.

Eddie's business goes so well that he has to hire someone to help him. That help is labor. The amount Eddie pays for help is called *wages*.

If Eddie purchases a machine to do the labor instead of a person, he is engaging in *automation*.

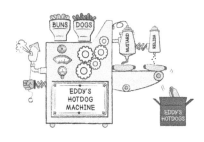

Mechanization and automation can lead to **UNEMPLOYMENT**.

Let's say that Eddie's competitor lowers his price to lure away Eddie's customers through **UNDERSELLING**.

If Eddie also lowers his prices, it can lead to a **PRICE WAR**. During a price war, profits *diminish*.

As part of Eddie's costs, the government charges him for the right to sell hot dogs. This is called a **TAX**.

If Polly Purchaser wants to buy part of Eddie's business, he will sell her some **STOCK**.

Eddie hopes that people will like his hot dogs a lot. If they do, maybe someday someone will want to buy the right to sell them in other cities all over the world. This is called a **FRANCHISE**.

How was that for a whirlwind tour of economics? Now that we have a grasp of the basics, let's dive into the deep end of the pool and explore some of the more complex economic concepts.

5

SCARCITY, CHOICE,
AND COST

E arlier I pointed out that economics isn't just about collecting economic data and producing matrices to predict future conditions. It's about people. Every culture is composed of people with their complex emotions, behaviors, and beliefs. Culture affects economics, and in turn, a government's chosen system of economics impacts culture and the individuals within that culture.

That's why I love the study of cultural economics. It looks beyond the analytical number crunching of the econometrics laboratory to the relationship between culture and economic outcomes. Cultural economics enables us to combine the basic principles of economics with the unpredictable thoughts, choices, and behaviors of more than seven billion people on the earth today. It can send us on an exciting adventure that opens our eyes to the motives, methods, successes, and failures in managing the world's resources and reveals how traditions, institutions, religious beliefs, and values can influence economic and political systems.

I like to think of economics as the study of making good choices under conditions of scarcity or abundance. In the pages that follow, we'll learn about the economic trilogy of scarcity, choice, and cost and discover how we can make good choices in our quest to become better off.

Scarcer Than Hens' Teeth

When I was growing up, folks would use the phrase "scarcer than hens' teeth" when something was really difficult to find. And everybody seemed to know how scarce hens' teeth were.

But when I began to study economics, I learned that *scarcity* has a slightly different meaning. Instead of relating to things that are hard to find, it refers to *any commodity that has at least two alternative uses*. A commodity is considered scarce only when we can figure out more uses for it than the commodity itself can supply.

According to the model of scarcity, our desires and demands for the things we can produce from commodities are limitless, but our resources are limited. Thus, we live in a world of scarcity. There is just so much of something and no more. In the end, the scarcity model raises some challenging questions:

- How will a commodity be used?
- Who will produce something from the commodity and distribute it?
- What product(s) will be made from the commodity?
- How and for whom should the goods and services be produced?
- When a commodity is used to produce something, can it be replaced or duplicated?
- Can a commodity be recycled for another go-round?

It's intriguing to observe how people answer these questions. Everybody would like to have more and better everything, so our unlimited wants are forever colliding with the limits of our resources, forcing us to pick some alternatives and reject others. The question of scarcity is ultimately a question of *cultural economics* because it involves people and their behavior.

When our Jackson Brothers Investments company was involved in real-estate development in the ski areas of Colorado in the 1960s and 1970s, we owned a motel right in the middle of Winter Park village on US Route 40. We wanted to build a post office on that land so we'd always have a say about future development in the village. We also knew the value of the property surrounding the post office would permanently increase. But we couldn't use the land for a post office and other development projects if the motel continued to fill the space.

At that point, the highway property on ten acres in the middle of the village became a scarce commodity. It had at least two viable alternative uses. Other people were also knocking on our door wanting to buy the property for their own projects.

We faced a giant dilemma. On the one hand, the motel was giving us cash flow, and if we tore it down, the income would stop. On the other hand, we wanted to increase property value and retain a say in future development.

So what did we do? You're right. We demolished the hotel, hauled off the debris, built the post office, and lived happily ever after.

You and I wrestle with the economics of scarcity every day of our lives. Time is a scarce commodity in today's world, and we have unlimited demands on each precious segment. Do I go to the gym next Tuesday after work or get the oil changed in my car?

It seems that virtually everything in our world is scarce. We used to consider the space above the earth as a free commodity because it seems to go on forever. But conflicts are now arising over the allocation of orbital slots (pathways used for orbiting the earth). The space in space is apparently becoming a scarce commodity for our telecommunication satellites. Even commercial airlines are squabbling over new and improved "highways in the skies."

The force of gravity that keeps us tethered to the earth would appear to be one of the only remaining examples of a totally free commodity, since almost everything else we think of is considered a scarce commodity simply because the supply is limited and we have unlimited desires and demands.

It's My Choice

Scarcity moves into the realm of cultural economics when choice enters the picture. The reality of limited resources and unlimited desires and needs presents us with a troublesome dilemma. Even though we live in a culture of excessive demands and unbelievable entitlement, we don't always get everything we want. It seems that the uses for a particular resource will always exceed the supply. Our *want to* always gets beat up by our *can do*.

The simple answer to the sticky-wicket issue of limited resources is that we ultimately have to make *choices*. As I pointed out earlier, economics is the study of making *good* choices. Wouldn't you like to know how to make good choices so that your life would be better and more fulfilling? Wouldn't it be nice if our culture, including our government, could learn how to make informed, responsible choices so that everyone could have the opportunity to become better off?

In a world of scarce resources, choices can become difficult and complex not only for individuals and families but for corporations, communities, national governments, and international organizations. In fact, choices are *inherently* complex because they are so closely connected to values. What you value most will ultimately determine your individual choices. And a conflict in values among the various individuals and groups in a culture only adds to the complexity.

There will always be tension between limited resources and unlimited desires and demands. And the choices we make typically come with a hitch: *when we say yes to one thing, we must say no to the alternatives.* It's as simple as that.

Would you rather purchase a home in a congested, trouble-ridden neighborhood close to work or own a home with a few acres out in the country? You could enjoy a better quality of life in the country, with plenty of space to raise your family, but it would also mean spending all your time commuting, and you'd arrive home after your family has gone to bed.

We can't escape choices in life. The question is whether we'll make good choices between the various alternatives available. And no matter which option we embrace, we'll inevitably experience consequences for our choices.

In my county in Colorado, for example, residents are passionate about preserving an unencumbered view of a lovely snow-covered mountain. So they petitioned the county's open-space committee to purchase the land that will preserve their view. That choice, however, comes at a cost: no homes can be built in the entire valley.

Naturally, the preservation mentality becomes contagious and ignites a race to protect everyone's view of every beautiful, snow-covered mountain in Colorado. The taste of victory is short lived, however, when folks discover that choices have consequences. Gradually it dawns on them that to preserve those coveted mountain views, they've removed 45 percent of the open real estate in the county from property-tax rolls, eliminated the possibility of future residential and commercial development, and forfeited the revenue necessary to pay the bills. But the views are spectacular.

Our Obsession with Cost

One of the most interesting aspects of our present consumer culture is our fixation with price. The burning question seems to be "What does it cost?" The price of a product is typically reflected on a bar code or price tag, but the money we hand the cashier may not reflect the actual cost.

Stores are quick these days to tempt shoppers with price rollbacks and reductions "for a limited time only." Everywhere we turn, sales ads call out to us, "Hurry! Don't miss out!" The pressure to buy can be overpowering, and we can find our resistance growing weak as we struggle to make good decisions. But retailers have figured out how to play the game. When it comes to cost, they have effectively narrowed the logic of our decisions to the question, "Do I have enough money to buy this?"

In today's culture, however, a convenient piece of plastic in your wallet nullifies that logic and allows you to make the purchase anyway. You walk away fully confident that you did the really smart thing because you simply couldn't have lived without the item another day at that irresistible price. I actually know folks who will drive all the way across town to purchase gasoline if the price is one cent per gallon cheaper than the competition. They spend three dollars to get across town to save twenty-four cents at the pump. *But what was the real cost?*

Our modern-day thinking regarding price tags often fails to consider the real cost. In the discipline of economics, cost is viewed through a different pair of glasses. It isn't determined by how much money we spend or how many plastic swipes we transact. Cost is inexorably linked to scarcity and choice. In fact, scarcity, choice, and cost are at the very heart of the study of economics.

When a good or service is considered scarce, choosing one alternative means we forgo the next highest alternative. The very existence of alternative uses of a resource forces us to make choices. The *opportunity cost* of any choice is the value of the next best alternative that was lost or forfeited in making the choice. The *true* cost of the alternative that wasn't chosen may have nothing at all to do with the advertised price of the product.

Here are just a few illustrations of lost-opportunity cost:

- A university student gives up four years of earned income and pays thousands of dollars to attend university classes, which he hopes will better his position for the balance of his life.
- A girl gives up marrying her childhood sweetheart to pursue a music career in London.
- A farmer decides to continue farming the old family acreage instead of selling the property to a big-box store.

I need look no further for real-life examples of scarcity, choice, and cost than my friends at Project C.U.R.E. More than seventeen thousand Project C.U.R.E. volunteers work at various warehouses and collection sites around the United States, and each of those volunteers can tell you a personal story of scarcity, choice, and cost. The stories are packed with drama and passion because they represent personal desires and values. These committed folks faithfully volunteer by the scores—but at a cost.

In 1999, an operating-room nurse named Barb Youngberg toured our Project C.U.R.E. facility in Denver with a friend. She was so intrigued by what she saw, she decided to volunteer one night a month sorting medical supplies.

Gradually Barb began donating more of her time, even after she retired from her hospital job in 2005. In 2007, doctors discovered that Barb had congestive heart failure and performed open-heart surgery, which included inserting a pacemaker. As Barb spent the next two and a half weeks in rehab, she knew she had a huge decision to make. She realized that the remaining years of her life were a scarce commodity. What would she do with those years? Would she take some leisure cruises or relax around home or what?

Barb realized that what she wanted most of all was to continue volunteering with Project C.U.R.E. *She decided to give the best of her life for the rest of her life helping other people become better off.*

Barb volunteered to take over the entire biomedical-technology area at Project C.U.R.E.'s new facility in Centennial, Colorado, and agreed to manage not only the inventory but lots of people who would be helping her build and run an efficient department. During her career as a nurse, Barb had accumulated valuable experience working with biomed-tech equipment, so when X-ray units, defibrillators, and other machines arrived at Project C.U.R.E.'s docks, she knew exactly how to get that lifesaving equipment ready for shipment to hospitals and clinics around the world.

Faced with the *scarcity* of years, Barb Youngberg *chose* to help save countless lives around the world at the *cost* of her next highest alternatives—cruises and leisure time. I salute Barb for fifteen years of voluntary service with Project C.U.R.E. and her determination to make good choices.

The Weakness of the Trilogy

The scarcity, choice, and cost trilogy pops up very early in life.

"Do you want Mommy to continue rocking you?" Baby nods yes. "Then stop crying."

When Junior reaches a certain age, Mommy sets out two outfits of clothing on the bed and says, "Which outfit do you want to wear today?"

Later Mommy asks, "Which toy do you want to take in the car—your teddy bear or your fire truck?"

When Junior is old enough, Mommy teaches him how to play Monopoly, a game that's based on scarcity, choice, and cost. There are limited houses, hotels, and money to go around in the game, and like poker, one player ends up with more, while the other players end up with less. Monopoly is a *zero-sum game*: the only way one player can win is at the expense of someone else.

It's like an apple pie: if one person gets more, another person gets less.

Over the years, our culture has bought into the economic concept of scarcity, choice, and cost to such a degree that it has become an axiomatic factor of life. There is only so much, and there is nothing more. We really have accepted that we live in a closed economy. If you have something, it's because someone else doesn't. You took it away from someone else, or you wouldn't have more. This is the *scarcity model*.

Economic models were developed to make simplified *general* assumptions about some aspect of the real world. These simplified assumptions, however, don't necessarily reflect the conditions in the real world. The trilogy of scarcity, choice, and cost is a wonderful mechanism *if used as designed*, but its assumptions may not be based in reality.

In my opinion, we have slipped over the edge of reason if we think that *everything* must fit the scarcity model. That is both sad and dangerous. Just because the rooster crows before the dawn doesn't mean the rooster wakes up the sun.

It's simplistic to assume that the reason we have an abundance of poor people in the world is because a few other people have grabbed a huge portion of the pie and left everyone else empty handed. Assuming that we have a closed economy in which all resources are deficient or depleted tends to promote zero-sum thinking. Remember: in a zero-sum game, the only way one person can benefit is if another person loses. That's a circular trap.

When we allow the scarcity model to convince us that zero-sum economics is always the result, then our future decisions will be adversely skewed. We are robbed of the possibility of growth and no longer employ creativity and imagination to solve problems by discovering new resources to meet our needs. Instead, we spend all our time and efforts trying to "make do" with the limited resources we think we have. At that point, we get caught up in a redistribution mentality, convinced that those who have all the resources should divide them equally with those who don't.

We can easily fall into the trap of thinking that Middle Eastern charlatans control all the energy resources, and one day those resources will simply dry up. We tend to focus on predicting and preparing for what will happen when scarcity finally catches up with us rather than exploring and developing new sources of energy.

It's important to keep in mind that *the net result of scarcity is poverty, and the net result of poverty is dependency.* If we live in a world of scarcity, choice, and cost alone, it will surely become a self-fulfilling prophecy. Everything will indeed become truly scarce, and poverty will be the bitter result.

After years of international travel, I've come to believe that the problem of scarcity can be overcome, and the cycle of poverty can be broken. One effective strategy has been the phenomenon of microcredit. The idea germinated in Bangladesh in 1976 when the Grameen Bank began offering small loans at low interest rates to the poor in rural areas.[1] The program became a popular tool for economic development, sparking a revolution in micro-entrepreneurship, generating employment, and creating real wealth throughout the developing world. The majority of microcredit recipients today are women, who now have an opportunity to establish a sustainable means of income. When their enterprises grow, disposable income increases, which leads to more economic growth and development. The results of this model are the exact opposite of zero-sum economics.

Microenterprise owners don't have more because others in their villages have less. Everyone becomes better off. What a glorious experience it is to see the cycle of debilitating poverty being broken, and people being given an opportunity to become part of the solution.

6

★ ★ ★

THE MECHANICS
OF CHANGE

It's relatively easy to see that economic and cultural choices trigger change, and change in turn influences economic and cultural outcomes. But how exactly does this happen?

As we've already discussed, cultural economics is the study of how culture, with its traditions, institutions, belief systems, and values, influences economic systems, and how economic systems impact and shape culture. Anytime those cultural and economic factors intersect, we can count on change. As I've said before, *transformation takes place at the intersection of culture and economics*. If we're good detectives, we can not only figure out why change happens, but we can also learn to predict it in some instances. It's pretty intriguing stuff, don't you think?

We live in a world where changes are continually taking place. I'm personally intrigued with the *mechanics of change*, or how change happens. Yet most of us are so caught up in the everyday affairs of life that we fail to recognize change when it's occurring. When we look back and compare the present with the way life used to be, it dawns on us that something has changed. But we aren't sure why or how. We simply realize that the form, nature, content, or course of something is now different from what it once was, or from what it would have been if everything had remained the same. That's change.

As a cultural economist, I've disciplined myself to look for change as it's happening. In my work with Project C.U.R.E. around the world, I've had abundant opportunities to observe firsthand a broad spectrum of change. Transformation can occur slowly and unobtrusively, or it can erupt suddenly in seismic grandeur. Change can take place individually, corporately, regionally, nationally, internationally, and even cosmically. We can count on change. And as I noted earlier, we can anticipate change whenever cultural and economic factors come together.

So just how does transformation take place? Let's hang out at the curbside for a bit and observe the factors that converge at the intersection of culture and economics to bring about this amazing phenomenon we call change.

The Economic Building Blocks of Change

When economists talk about the "components of production," they're typically referring to four traditional categories of economic resources: land, labor, capital, and the entrepreneur. These are the economic building blocks of change.

1. *Land.* Simply stated, *land* is God's gift to humankind (see Psalm 115:16). It is the earth in its unaltered natural state. As an economic concept, it includes everything on, above, and below the surface of the earth, including streams, lakes, minerals, forests, air, space, wild animals, plants, fossil fuels, and even asteroids from outer space. Land essentially refers to everything we find in our environment that isn't a product of our labor.

It's important to remember three points about land and other natural resources:

    a. They exist in nature.

    b. No human effort was involved in making or altering them.

    c. They can be used to produce goods and services.

2. *Labor.* The physical and mental talents we use to produce goods and services are considered labor. Anyone who performs a productive function is engaging in labor, including airline pilots, teachers, welders, retail clerks, mechanics, professional football players, or even rocket scientists. Generally speaking, labor is an individual's most useful and powerful resource. When economists refer to the *free*

labor market or *competitive labor market*, they simply mean that individuals can voluntarily exchange or sell their labor power in the marketplace to the highest bidder. The bidder, in turn, can exchange or purchase labor power at the best terms he or she can find.

3. *Capital.* In economics, capital consists of anything that enhances production. It essentially comprises the wealth—or goods—used to produce more wealth. Capital goods aren't the final product but are employed in the production process. Money, however, isn't considered a basic economic resource, since it produces nothing by itself.[1] Examples of capital include factories, warehouses, distribution centers, office buildings, and transportation facilities, as well as tools and equipment, such as wrenches, drill presses, industrial robots, printers, computers, and other pieces of machinery. Economists refer to the purchase of capital goods as *capital investment.* Capital goods differ from consumer goods because consumer goods satisfy desires or needs directly, whereas capital goods do so indirectly by assisting in the production of consumer goods and services.

4. *The entrepreneur.* Entrepreneurs are the agents of change. As the driving force behind production, they take the initiative to combine the resources of land, labor, and capital to produce goods and services. Nothing in business happens without entrepreneurs. In a very real sense, an entrepreneur is both a spark plug, which ignites an action, and an epoxy, which keeps the components of an action glued together. The time, effort, and abilities entrepreneurs invest in a business endeavor are no guarantee of success or profit, however. The risks entrepreneurs accept may result in losses rather than rewards, and those risks may involve not only their own assets but the assets of associates and stockholders as well.

Students sometimes struggle with the concept of *entrepreneurship.* It's a tricky word to spell and pronounce, but perhaps the simplest way to understand this term is to remember that all an entrepreneur really does is take something of lesser value out of the economic system and return it to the system at a higher value.

For example, when I was a partner at Jackson Brothers Investments, my brothers and I performed the very simple and rewarding task of taking struggling ranches out of the economy and developing them into beautiful recreational and business sites in Colorado's ski country. The ranches were contributing almost no tax revenue to the county or state, but we were able to return the redeveloped sites to the economy at a much higher value.

I'm also very proud of the work Project C.U.R.E. has done to take surplus medical goods out of our economic system, where they were just sitting on shelves collecting dust, and reinsert them into the international economy, where they are being used to save thousands of lives.

The components of land, labor, capital, and the entrepreneur serve an essential function in production and wealth creation by contributing to the satisfaction (or *utility* in economic terms) that people derive from the goods and services they consume. In other words, the effective use of our economic resources makes people very happy.

The Cultural Building Blocks of Change

Now let's examine the cultural components of change. The word *culture* sometimes conjures images of art exhibits in glitzy museums or microorganisms in a laboratory petri dish. But that isn't what I'm talking about here. Culture, as we discussed earlier, consists of the shared beliefs, attitudes, emotions, values, customs, ideals, and social behaviors of any group of people. (I'd love to share with you some of the intriguing customs and traditions I've observed in my world travels, but that's the subject of another book).

There are four strategic components of culture: traditions, institutions, the family, and the individual.

1. *Traditions.* The word *tradition* comes from the Latin word *tradere*, which means "to transmit, to hand over, to give for safekeeping." Traditions are valued beliefs or patterns of behavior with special or symbolic meanings that have been

handed down from generation to generation and may evolve over thousands of years. The concept carries with it the notion of holding on to a previous time.

Certain religious traditions, such as circumcision and welcoming the Sabbath (Shabbat) date back thousands of years. Examples of cultural traditions include national holidays and anthems, citizenship rites, special foods and clothing, the languages people speak, and the place of women in domestic affairs. Societal traditions may be reflected in the ways people greet one another (i.e., saying hello and thank you) and how they perform wedding ceremonies. Political traditions can be as simple as the labels or distinctions we assign to various groups, such as *right wing* and *left wing*. Throughout history, wars have been fought and people have even laid down their lives for their traditions.

2. *Institutions.* The role of an institution is to formalize and perpetuate the agreed-upon rules and traditions that govern the social behavior of a group of people. Institutions supply the structure, organization, influence, and authority necessary to sustain the traditions people value most highly.

We typically think of churches, hospitals, prisons, banks, and schools as institutions. But they are merely the visible physical representations of religious, medical, judicial, financial, and educational systems. These surface structures describe the underlying *normative systems* (how things ought to be) that regulate the distribution of goods and services, facilitate the legitimate use of power, transmit knowledge to the next generation, and provide a social framework for moral and religious matters.

3. *The family.* In the twenty-first century, the concept of family has evolved beyond the traditional view and now incorporates seemingly endless configurations. For the purposes of this discussion, whenever I refer to the family, I'm talking about kinship relationships and the essential role they play in change at the intersection of culture and economics. Although the family consists of the basic social unit of parents and their children, it extends to any group of persons closely related by blood, including parents, children, grandparents, uncles, aunts, and cousins.

Historically, kinship has played a significant role in developing, establishing, and perpetuating traditions. The family unit is perhaps the most powerful influence in perpetuating and sustaining institutions.

4. *The individual.* Of all the components of culture, the individual emerges as the ultimate building block of change. The individual—like the entrepreneur in business—is an agent of change. Nothing happens in a culture without the initiative and influence of the individual. Without getting mired in a philosophical discourse on the subject—empiricism, existentialism, Buddhism, and even Ayn Rand's objectivism would present different views—I would simply contend that the individual is the pinnacle of God's creation, carefully designed and fashioned in God's own image. Alone, each of us represents the smallest minority on earth, but when it comes to our ability to exercise our freedom to choose, individuals are also the largest majority on the planet. It's enigmatic to think that one individual can alter the course of history, but it's true. Consider some examples of individuals who changed the world for the better.

Mother Teresa	Florence Nightingale
Mahatma Gandhi	Mozart, Handel, and Beethoven
Marie Curie	Harriet Tubman
Jesus Christ	Johannes Gutenberg
Margaret Thatcher	Helen Keller
George Washington Carver	Albert Einstein

The Matrix

The eight components we just discussed converge in amazingly diverse and intricate ways at the intersection of economics and culture to bring about the phenomenon of change. This collision of cultural and economic factors forms a *cultural-economic matrix*. At the exact point where these factors cross at the intersection of real life, transformation occurs.

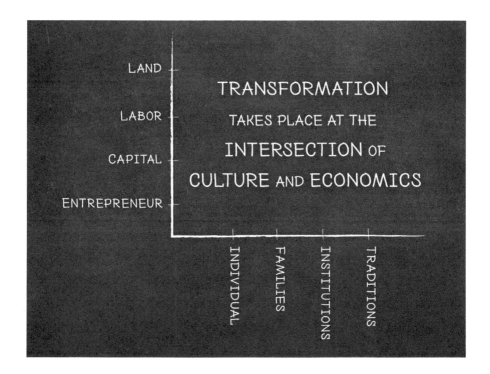

Let's walk through a few examples to see how the matrix works. In the following chalkboard diagrams, you'll notice that the economic components of land,
labor, capital, and the entrepreneur line up along the left side of the matrix. The
cultural components of traditions, institutions, the family, and the individual line up
along the bottom. The key dynamics of each scenario determine the point at which
economic and cultural components intersect to trigger change.

First, let's return to America in 1776, when a fledgling nation engaged in an epic
war against a tyrannical British king for liberty and the right of self-government. The
revolutionary vision of the American colonists could not be squelched. They fought
and died to secure their God-given rights to "life, liberty, and the pursuit of happiness." At the intersection of culture and economics, traditions, institutions, and
families collided head-on with issues of land, labor, and capital. The result? A free
and independent nation founded on the principles of liberty, the rule of law, and
the opportunity to become better off.

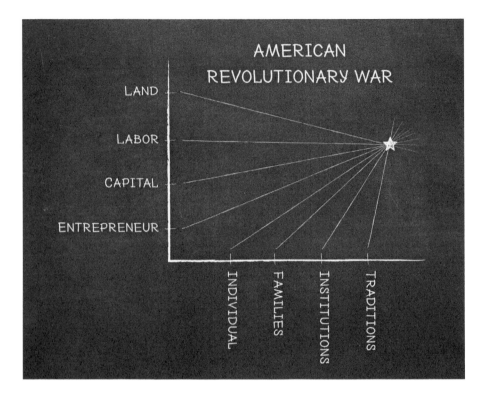

Next, let's consider a modern-day example. China has experienced immeasurable cultural and economic transformation as a result of the government's one-child policy. This policy, which took effect in 1979 and has only recently been overturned,[2] allowed Chinese couples to bear and raise only one child. Those who violated the policy risked stiff penalties, as well as forced abortions or sterilizations. The policy was originally instituted to control population growth, which had exploded under Mao Zedong in the 1950s, and to conserve the nation's vulnerable food supply. It was also purported to alleviate many other social, economic, and environmental problems.[3]

As an incentive to conform to the policy, couples with just one child received government benefits and awards. Unfortunately, since male babies were valued more than females, baby girls were often killed or ended up in orphanages.[4] I personally visited many orphanages throughout China and witnessed firsthand the destructive impact of this policy.

As the key economic components of land, labor, and capital converged with the cultural components of traditions, institutions, families, and individuals, a firestorm of change was unleashed in China as a consequence of the one-child policy.

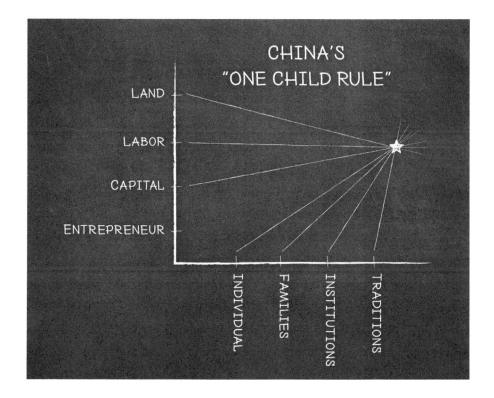

Finally, let's look at an example a little closer to home. Over the years, controversial land-use issues, such as eminent domain, have caused major transformations in communities around the United States. Government institutions endeavor to dictate how certain pieces of property will be used, regardless of individual or corporate ownership rights. Municipalities, for instance, may attempt to appropriate or condemn a property so others can build a big-box store or commercial shopping strip to generate higher tax revenues. The key components of land, labor, and the entrepreneur collide with traditions, institutions, families, and individuals as the battle is waged at the intersection of culture and economics.

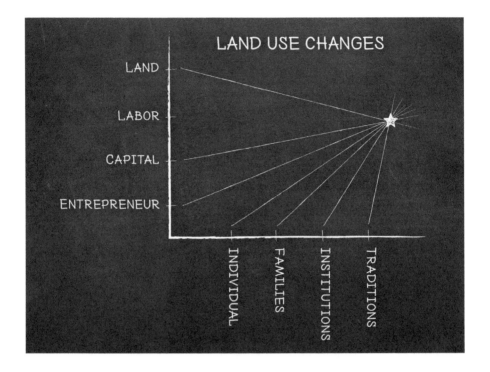

When we recognize the cultural and economic components involved in change and understand how those factors interact, we not only learn to anticipate change better, but we become more efficient in allocating and managing our resources. And as we'll see, we all have an important role to play in this grand drama at the intersection of culture and economics.

Market Baskets

Each of us is standing on the curbside of the intersection where transformation happens. From that vantage point, we observe the constant flow of traffic moving through the intersection. But we aren't just standing on the curbside as disengaged and disinterested observers. We, along with everyone else gathered there, are highly involved in determining not only what passes through that intersection but what the results will be. Transformation continually takes place in the world around us, and we are a part of it.

If we observe carefully, we'll see that everyone standing on the curbside is carrying a lovely market basket filled with valuable items they have been gathering along the way. The items are precious because individuals have exchanged part of themselves for what they collected, either through a direct purchase or a gift exchange. The contents of those market baskets are powerful enough to direct and alter the course of history.

Since each of us plays such an important role in the ultimate course of history, perhaps we should take a peek inside our market baskets and see what they contain.

As you inventory the contents of your basket, you'll likely discover that they fall into five categories:

1. *Financial possessions*—This category includes savings accounts, cash, loans and sums others owe you, stocks, bonds, pension plans, business equities, partnerships, homes and other properties, autos, and household goods, minus any debts you owe.

2. *Personal possessions*—These include both tangible and intangible individual possessions—separate from financial and spiritual possessions—such as your health, DNA and other physical attributes, attitudes, intellectual capacities, past experiences, education, emotional characteristics, decision-making capabilities, and temporal possessions (i.e., the number of days you estimate that you have left on this earth).

3. *Relational possessions*—Your relationships with family and friends are included in this category, along with your influence on people and situations.

4. *Spiritual possessions*—This category includes your relationship with God, as well as your spiritual attributes. Is your life characterized by joy, love, peace, and other qualities that flow from your spiritual core? Are you self-controlled, patient, and kind toward others? Do you practice forgiveness and gratitude?

5. *Special possessions*—In addition to the other possessions in your market basket, God has given you some special gifts, talents, and abilities. Although you may have put a lot of work and discipline into developing them, you realize they're special possessions you received as gifts.

As you gaze into your market basket and examine the contents, a probing question awaits your response: "What'cha gonna do with what'cha got?" You have the power to choose which contents to take from your market basket and inject into the flow of traffic at the intersection of culture and economics. So choose wisely and remember: your curbside choices will ultimately influence the course of history.

WHAT IS MONEY?

Most of us think of money as the cash in our bank accounts or the change in our pockets, but as we'll see in this chapter, money is so much more than dollars and cents. It's important to understand the nature of money in order to see how it relates to economics and culture.

So what is money? Where did it come from, and who determines its value? Do credit cards and virtual currencies qualify as money? What happens if people lose confidence in its value?

Eighteenth-century philosopher and economist David Hume clarified what money is by stating what it isn't:

> Money is not, properly speaking, one of the subjects of commerce; but only the instrument which men have agreed upon to facilitate the exchange of one commodity for another. It is none of the wheels of trade: It is the oil which renders the motions of the wheels more smooth and easy.[1]

According to Hume, money is simply an *instrument* to facilitate trade. In other words, it is the means we use to engage in commerce.

Currency (as in dollars and cents) certainly qualifies as money, but money can be anything people *value* as wealth and agree to use as a medium of exchange. People will always fabricate some form of money to facilitate trading the things they have for the things they want. It might be possible to imagine a cashless society, but not a moneyless society.

Confidence and *convenience* determine what is commonly relied upon as money. If a more convenient medium of exchange comes along that can still retain people's confidence, it has the potential to become a new form of money. Whenever people lose confidence in the purchasing power of whatever they're using as money, that medium then ceases to be money.

The Bitcoin is one example of a new form of money called "virtual currency." Whether it survives as a legitimate and convenient medium of exchange with purchasing power that people can place their confidence in has yet to be seen. Other forms of virtual money, such as PayPal, are becoming increasingly popular and may eventually edge out the dollar and plastic money like debit cards and credit cards, a phenomenon of my generation.

Although money can be anything of value that people agree to use as a medium of exchange in the marketplace, it must play by the universal rules of economics. Ultimately *confidence* trumps convenience. For money to fulfill its role as the "oil" that lubricates the "wheels of trade," those who use it must have sufficient confidence in its stability and reliability.

A Thumbnail History of Money

In my worldwide travels over the years, I've observed different cultures using some pretty strange articles as money, such as salt, animal hides, wives, cattle or chickens, wheat, beads, and even eggs. Historically, however, metal has been the most common form of money. It's a whole lot easier to make change with pieces of metal than with raw eggs.

Economist Adam Smith lauded metal currency in the mid-1700s:

Metals can not only be kept with as little loss as any other commodity, scarce any thing being less perishable than they are, but they can likewise, without any loss, be divided into any number of parts, as by fusion those parts can easily be re-united again; a quality which no other equally durable commodities possess, and which, more than any other quality, renders them fit to be the instruments of commerce and circulation.[2]

But over the centuries, it became inconvenient to stand in line at the marketplace, pull out a bar of gold, whack off a bit, and weigh it accurately to pay for a purchase. So coins became more convenient to use. Minted coins were easy to identify and often bore the image and guarantee of some government leader. Governments like to control monetary systems, so they typically take over the minting of coins. In the United States, under the Coinage Act of 1792—also known as the Mint Act—it became illegal for an individual to debase, or reduce the value of, metal coins, and doing so was considered a crime punishable by death. This act has survived *almost* intact until the present. (You won't get the hangman's rope for debasing currency today.)

Eventually the desire for convenience motivated people to use pieces of paper as money instead of lugging around bags of heavy metal bars or clumsy coins. That required a gigantic leap of confidence, since people had to trust that others would accept their paper money as payment for goods and services or to satisfy debts.

In the beginning, paper money looked more like a receipt. For safety and convenience, people would take their gold or silver to a business that was equipped to store precious metals—such as a goldsmith's shop—or they might place their metal in a local bank vault for "safekeeping." The goldsmith or banker would then give the depositor a receipt of ownership for the metal. When the depositor wanted to make a purchase or pay a debt, he would simply sign the receipt and hand it over to a new owner—a bit like signing over a car title. The new owner could then exchange his receipt at the bank or goldsmith's shop for possession of the actual metal. Or he might simply sign the receipt over to another person when making a purchase or paying a debt.

The first paper money in America came not from banks but from the new colonial governments. In 1690, instead of issuing a tangible asset like gold or silver, Massachusetts issued paper money backed only with a promise to redeem it. Soon the market was flooded with junk paper money, which people used to purchase available goods. The result? Prices soared. Paper money drove metal coins out of circulation simply because everyone began hoarding them. By 1751, Britain prohibited the printing or issuing of any more paper money.

When the Mint Act of 1792 was passed in America, the dollar was adopted as the standard unit of currency. What tangible asset backed up the dollar? Gold. At least until President Roosevelt and the US Congress abandoned the gold standard domestically in 1933. Roosevelt also signed an executive order requiring citizens to turn over to the new Federal Reserve System any "hoarded" gold, with limited exceptions.[3] Afterward, people continued to place their confidence in the dollar because they believed that every dollar in circulation was backed by one dollar's worth of gold in Fort Knox, Kentucky.

That was nothing but a sick joke. In 1950, US gold reserves totaled $22.8 billion, but by early 1972, they had plummeted to $10.2 billion, a decrease of more than $12 billion.[4] To make matters worse, foreign governments demanded that the United States repay its trade imbalances in gold. So for every dollar issued, there was less than one penny in gold reserves.

On August 15, 1971, President Richard Nixon severed the link between international currency and real gold, and the United States began to pay its international debts in dollars. The world has accepted the dollar as the international standard of payment ever since.

Once paper money was accepted as a medium of exchange, paper checks eventually followed, also based on confidence and convenience. The practice of writing checks is a throwback to the receipt system in which a depositor signed over the receipt for his precious metal to someone else. Paper checks allow a depositor to authorize the safekeeper of his wealth (such as a bank) to transfer funds from one account to another as a means of payment. As long as the intended recipient of the funds is convinced she'll actually end up with the funds, she'll accept the written check as money.

When credit cards appeared on the scene in the 1920s, they weren't seen as real money because they required another form of money, either cash or check, to pay off the monthly charges. But the convenience of plastic money was so alluring and addictive that consumers hardly gave the confidence factor a second thought. Oil companies and hotels initially issued credit cards to customers, and by 1950 Diners Club issued the first multipurpose credit card.[5] Eventually, plastic money evolved to include debit cards, which authorized an immediate transfer of wealth from the cardholder to the merchant through a financial institution.

As I touched on earlier, virtual or digital currency has entered the marketplace in recent years as yet another form of money. The Bitcoin is just one example. Convenience is king in our culture, and using tangible money is increasingly seen as both a nuisance and nescience. But placing absolute confidence in a collection of numbers stored in a computer and assuming our virtual money is safe is just wishful thinking.

Confidence and convenience ultimately determine what people accept as money. But virtual currency may turn out to be a case of misplaced confidence in a world where money has become an ethereal concept rather than a tangible asset. That's a scary and vulnerable position for any culture to be in.

8

BANK ON IT

As we learned in the previous chapter, money isn't what it used to be. It has morphed over time because of our demand for convenience. Money is now a concept rather than a tangible asset. We no longer think of it as a bar of gold or silver from which we peel off enough shavings to pay the bills. It's simply a credit or debit stored in the memory chip of some computer and backed up solely by the confidence that someone else will accept our ethereal money as payment for what we owe.

Just as our concept of money has slowly changed over time, so has the world of banking. Today when you deposit money in a bank, you enter into an agreement in which the bank promises to return your money upon demand, either immediately if you have a checking account or within a few months if you have a savings account. The majority of money you deposit in the bank is loaned to others who may not be required to repay it for twenty or thirty years. Obviously the bank can't technically keep both agreements. History has proven, however, that if the element of *confidence* is present, new depositors will place more money in the bank, and out of those new deposits, you can expect your money to be returned upon demand.

To protect you from a bank failure or loss of funds, the Federal Deposit Insurance Corporation (FDIC) guarantees your deposits up to $250,000. This is a promise the government only *presumes* it can keep. But it's designed to bolster confidence in the banking system and alleviate fears of depositing one's hard-earned money in a local bank.

In the following chapters, we'll learn more about how the banking system works, but right now, I'd like to weave a little tale to illustrate how the banking industry got its start. As you may recall, it essentially began when people started handing over their precious metals to goldsmiths and bankers for safekeeping. But as you'll see, there's much more to the story.

The Story of Banking—Part 1

Barney Businessman had accumulated a tidy sum of gold from his business dealings. Now he was confronted with the problem of keeping it safe. Because Gaffney Goldsmith worked with precious metals, he had constructed a thief-proof vault to protect his assets. So it was only natural that Barney went to Gaffney and asked to store his accumulated gold in Gaffney's vault. In fact, Barney told Gaffney that he was willing to pay a fee for the service.

When Barney deposited his gold in Gaffney's vault, he was given a *receipt of deposit*, which he had to present to Gaffney if he wanted to reclaim his gold. Other people in the community began to realize that Gaffney Goldsmith's vault was an extremely safe and convenient place to keep their gold as well. In fact, Gaffney's vault became somewhat of a warehouse for gold in the community.

Gaffney was a pretty intelligent fellow, so it didn't take him long to realize that on any given day, 80 to 90 percent of the gold in his vault simply sat there collecting dust. He became convinced that his customers would never withdraw all of their gold from his vault at the same time. Any daily withdrawals of gold would be offset by the deposit receipts Gaffney issued the same day when other customers deposited their gold in his vault. None of Gaffney's customers seemed to care whose gold they received when they wanted to make a withdrawal, so Gaffney usually withdrew gold from the few bags at the front of his vault, while all the bags in the back sat there collecting dust and taking up a lot of valuable vault space. Gaffney pondered this and realized that he had a good thing going.

The gold was an *asset* to Gaffney because it was under his control. The deposit receipts were a *liability* to him because they represented the owners' claims on the gold and, sooner or later the gold would have to be returned to the rightful owners. But Gaffney was always able to keep his books balanced.

GAFFNEY GOLDSMITH			
	Assets	Liabilities and Net Worth	
Gold	$2,000	Deposit Receipts	$2,000

Question: How might Gaffney Goldsmith generate more money and still keep his books balanced?

The Story of Banking—Part 2

Fenwick Farmer wanted to purchase some equipment for his farm that would increase his earning potential and raise his standard of living. He asked his family for a loan, but they turned him down flat. So money was on his mind when he visited his old friend Gaffney Goldsmith one day. When Fenwick observed all the gold in Gaffney's vault just collecting dust, he had a brilliant idea. He asked Gaffney if he could borrow some of the dust-covered gold from the back of the vault. Fenwick, who was a reasonable man, even offered to pay a fee to use the gold. Now that was of *interest* to Gaffney.

Gaffney was an honest and forthright man, and he always wanted to make sure his books would balance. So he went to Barney Businessman, who owned some of the dust-covered gold in the back of the vault, and he explained that Fenwick Farmer was willing to pay a fee to use Barney's gold temporarily. When Fenwick repaid the original sum, he would render the additional fee, which would come from the increased proceeds he earned as a result of his farm improvements.

Barney agreed to the plan, and Fenwick signed a *promissory note* agreeing to return the gold with interest. Gaffney agreed to split the interest equally with Barney and assured Barney that if he needed some gold before Fenwick repaid his loan, one of the other depositors would surely be willing to lend Barney some of their unused gold on the same basis. Everybody was happy and better off. And Gaffney's books still balanced. (*Note:* The total assets remained the same; only the *form* of the assets in his bag changed. Now Gaffney had $1,500 in gold assets and an asset worth $500 in the form of a signed note.)

GAFFNEY GOLDSMITH

	Assets	Liabilities and Net Worth	
Gold	$1,500	Deposit Receipts	$2,000
Note	$500		
	$2,000		

Gaffney was still confident that his depositors would never withdraw all of their gold at the same time, so he began lending more and more of his gold reserve. Soon he was making so much money from lending out the gold that he began enticing depositors to place their gold in his vault for safekeeping by *paying* them instead of charging them. This strategy was the forerunner of our modern concept of *fractional reserve banking*. All Gaffney had to do was to keep enough gold supply on hand (a "fraction" of the total sum) to take care of each day's transactions.

The Story of Banking—Part 3

Fenwick Farmer discovered that even though he had signed a *promissory note* and borrowed the gold from Gaffney Goldsmith, he also needed a safe place to keep the gold until he actually purchased his farm equipment. Obviously the safest place to keep it was in Gaffney's vault, so Fenwick asked Gaffney if he could make a deposit. Gaffney agreed to keep Fenwick's gold in his vault and issued Fenwick a de-

posit receipt. Gaffney had no problem with this transaction because his books still balanced.

GAFFNEY GOLDSMITH			
	Assets	Liabilities and Net Worth	
Gold	$2,000	Deposit Receipts	$2,000
Fenwick Note	$500	Fenwick Deposit Recipt	$500
	$2,500		$2,500

When Gaffney examined his books more closely, he noticed that the Fenwick transaction had increased his total assets and liabilities from $2,000 to $2,500. Now he was curious about how this would affect the total economy of the community.

One of the purchases Fenwick intended to make was a new, larger farm wagon to haul his produce to market. Wiseman Wagonwright built the finest wagons that ever rolled on four wooden wheels, so Fenwick agreed to purchase one of his wagons. When it came time to pay for the wagon, Fenwick explained to Wiseman that he needed to make a trip across town to draw out enough gold from Gaffney's vault to pay him.

Wiseman assured Fenwick that the trip wasn't necessary, since he also kept his gold in Gaffney's vault. If Fenwick withdrew gold to pay for the new wagon, Wiseman would just have to make a trip across town to redeposit the gold later. Such an inconvenience.

Wiseman suggested that Fenwick either split his gold deposit receipt and give part of it to Wiseman or write an authorization for Gaffney to transfer gold from Fenwick's account to Wiseman's account. Thus, an ancient version of the modern-day checking account was born. (It's true! When I visited the site of ancient Babylon while working in Iraq, I was told that archaeologists discovered clay slabs and goldsmiths' receipts that had been used for check writing.)

As Gaffney Goldsmith entered the transaction between Fenwick and Wiseman into his books, he realized the real impact of this strategy. If Fenwick's deposit receipt could be used as money to purchase his farm equipment, then that receipt actually *became* money in addition to all the gold in Gaffney's vault. In other words, if the deposit receipts were used as money, then money was actually *created* whenever Gaffney made loans and issued deposit receipts. Eureka!

The ancient goldsmith was performing the same functions as our present banks:

- Taking in deposits
- Making loans
- Issuing and honoring deposit receipts that, in effect, became money

Perhaps you're wondering what would keep Gaffney Goldsmith from lending more money than his vault actually contained. And if he did, how would depositors get their money back?

That's where bank regulation enters the picture.

9

CENTRALIZED BANKING
TAKES CENTER STAGE

In a moment we'll see how Gaffney's depositors would be protected if Gaffney made more loans than he could cover with the gold stored in his vault. But first let's shift our focus to the burgeoning economy of America in the late 1700s. As the economy expanded, the fledgling US government quickly realized it needed to exert some control over the banking system. (All governments inevitably do reach that conclusion, by the way.) But repeated attempts to bridle the banks were frustrated in the face of a freedom-loving citizenry and a horde of independent bankers who feared monopolies and federal control over the money supply. "Wildcat banking" was prevalent at the time, and all the banks were scrambling to make a profit.

The banking system's version of the Wild West was short lived, however. Many banks failed due to undisciplined management, and multiple bank panics in the 1800s paved the way for the National Bank Act of 1864, which established a national currency and, you guessed it, *national banks*. Soon after, the United States adopted the *gold standard*, which was intended to stabilize the economy by making all forms of US currency redeemable with gold. But the Panic of 1907, commonly known as the Bankers' Panic, shook the US economy and the banking system to the core. A stock-market crisis triggered a run on the banks that quickly spread across the nation. In the aftermath of the crisis, the economy experienced a sharp downturn that lasted for more than a year.

In 1908, the National Monetary Commission was formed to assess the banking system and issued a report on its findings three years later. Congress debated the commission's proposals for a good two years before concluding that the lack of a central banking system was to blame for the nation's economic volatility. On December 23, 1913, Congress passed the Federal Reserve Act, and president Woodrow Wilson signed it into law. The era of centralized banking had dawned in the United States.

The Federal Reserve had a twofold purpose: (1) to exert control over the nation's entire money supply, and (2) to step in to protect depositors if any bank became overextended. The Fed, it was argued, would guarantee the people's confidence in the banking system once and for all.

Individual banks were very reluctant to create a strong central banking system in Washington, DC, or New York City, so the Federal Reserve Act was a bit of a compromise. The country would be divided into twelve districts, with each district containing a Federal Reserve Bank and additional branch banks. All banks with a "national bank" designation were required to join the Federal Reserve, but state banks only joined if they so desired.

Old, established banks had no desire to be under federal control, but they had lobbied Congress for government regulations that would limit competition and protect their profits. So when the market crashed in 1929 and panic ensued, they refused to come to the aid of the banks that encountered runs on their reserves. Perhaps these ulterior motives contributed to the failure of the Federal Reserve System to ward off the bank crashes and the Great Depression.

The Mysterious Fed

We hear a lot about the Federal Reserve, but most of us haven't a clue about what it is, what it does, or who runs it. So let's clear up some of the confusion here and now.

The Federal Reserve Act of 1913 established a central banking system commonly referred to as the Federal Reserve System. The Federal Reserve is an independent organization established as an impartial "referee" to oversee the banking system.

Barney Businessman or Fenwick Farmer couldn't simply walk into a Federal Reserve Bank and make a deposit or negotiate a loan. A Federal Reserve Bank is exclusively for bankers. And as a bankers' bank, it receives deposits, holds reserves, issues notes and currency, and clears checks. The US Treasury Department, for example, deposits the money it collects from taxation, fees, and other charges in a Federal Reserve Bank and then pays the government's bills from that account.

Supervising the Federal Reserve System is a board of seven governors—the Federal Reserve Board—appointed to serve fourteen-year terms. Although the Fed isn't under the direct control of Congress or the president of the United States, the president does appoint new members to fill vacancies on the board of governors. This exclusive board is headed by a chairperson who often testifies before Congress. Alan Greenspan and Ben Bernanke filled that role in the past, and most recently Janet Yellen was appointed as chairwoman.

Assisting the Federal Reserve Board are the Federal Advisory Council (FAC) and the Federal Open Market Committee (FOMC). The advisory council, which consists of twelve bank representatives, meets a minimum of four times a year to advise the Fed on a variety of economic issues, while the market committee, also with twelve members, is in charge of operating the open market, which includes buying and selling government securities. (We'll see the importance of the Federal Open Market Committee later when we discuss inflation.)

It's important to remember that the Federal Reserve Board has ultimate control over the US money supply. The board members, or governors, have the power to either increase or decrease the total amount of money in the system, including that collection of ethereal digital currency stored in computers. The US Treasury prints paper money and mints coins, but the Federal Reserve System alone is authorized to place them into circulation.

Understanding the methods the Fed uses to control the money supply can give us valuable insights into the causes and effects of perhaps the most serious threat to any economy—inflation.

Manipulating the Money Supply

There are three ways the Federal Reserve Board—that mysterious group of faceless folks—manipulates the money supply.

1. *Controlling the fractional reserve requirements throughout the banking system.* As we discussed earlier, Gaffney Goldsmith had to be careful not to lend out more gold than he had on hand in his vault. He (and his depositors) needed a safeguard to prevent that from happening, and a fractional reserve requirement would have done the trick. This regulation is used to control the volatile expansion of the money supply. To prevent this expansion, the Federal Reserve requires each lending institution to hold a certain percentage of its deposits in reserve, either in its own vaults or on deposit in one of the Federal Reserve Banks.

The Fed maintains the right to raise or lower the percentage of those reserves within congressional limits. Quite simply, if the Fed requires banks to retain a larger percentage of deposits (i.e., the fractional reserve requirement is increased), they have less money to lend, and the money supply tends to shrink. If, however, the reserve requirement is lowered (i.e., a smaller deposit percentage is held in reserve), the money supply tends to expand, and it's easier to borrow money from the bank. Every time a bank makes a loan, the money supply is expanded. This sounds advantageous, but if the money supply expands too quickly, it can pose a serious threat to the monetary system.

Suppose that Billy Banker has a 5 percent fractional reserve requirement for his bank. That means he must set aside 5 percent of his deposit transactions so he'll be able to pay any of his customers the total amount in their accounts should they desire to withdraw their assets. So for every $100 deposited, Billy Banker has to set aside $5 in reserve. Let's say that Billy has $10,000 in his bank. His reserve requirement is $500, which means he's free to lend out the balance of $9,500 and charge borrowers interest on their loans to make a profit.

One morning Carlton Contractor walks into the bank wanting a $9,500 loan for a building project. He signs the loan papers, and that note becomes an asset of Billy's bank. Billy sets up an account for Carlton and deposits the $9,500 loan proceeds into that account. When the deposit transaction is complete, $9,500 of new money has just been created. But the money expansion doesn't stop there.

Billy then sets aside $475—the required 5 percent reserve from the newly created money—which leaves him with $9,025 in excess reserves to be loaned out again to the public. This expansion of the money supply takes place regardless of whether the funds stay in one bank or are processed through many banks. Notice that if Billy Banker lends out the $9,025 of excess reserves, the original $10,000 will grow to $28,525 in two simple steps. Surely this would startle even Gaffney Goldsmith.

If the required reserve ratio is 5 percent, the original amount of money can be expanded *twenty times* if carried to the maximum limit. That means the original $10,000 can potentially become $200,000 in new money. As we'll discover in the next chapter, the expansion of the money supply is at the heart of inflation.

2. *Controlling the discount rate for banks.* Banks not only use their customers' money, but they also borrow money from the Fed so they can lend more money to their customers. The rate the Federal Reserve charges banks to borrow money is known as the *discount rate*. If the discount rate is *lowered*, it becomes more attractive for banks to borrow from the Fed. When the Fed lends money to banks, the money supply expands. If the Fed *increases* the discount rate, banks tend to borrow less from the Fed and therefore lend less money to their customers. The money supply also tends to shrink.

The *prime rate* is the rate of interest a bank charges its best customers, who have enough clout with the bank that they can expect privileged recognition, or they'll take their business elsewhere. The prime rate is largely determined by the Fed's discount rate and the customers' demand for money. If the prime rate is too high for our friend Billy Banker, he will be unable to borrow from the Fed. That means he'll either have to curtail lending to his customers at the expense of his profit or find other investors who will lend him the money at a reasonable rate.

3. *Monetizing the government's debt.* This practice and corresponding policies fall under the umbrella of the Federal Reserve Board's activities of buying or selling US Treasury notes and securities. When the government overspends and runs out of money, it can either raise taxes or borrow what it needs. Raising taxes is classified as *fiscal policy*, whereas taking out a loan falls under the Federal Reserve's *monetary policy*. But who could lend the government trillions of dollars to cover its extravagant spending? The answer is lots and lots of people.

The government borrows money by issuing Treasury bills (T-bills), notes, and security bonds to US citizens and foreign countries with a promise to repay the money in the future. When the time comes for the government to repay the loans, the Federal Reserve steps in and—voilà!—pays off the debts with newly created money.

Some people liken this practice to a Ponzi scheme, but it's more formally referred to as *monetizing the debt*. When the government monetizes its own debt, it turns that debt into spendable money. As we'll soon see, it's the most spurious and oblique method the Fed uses to manipulate the money supply.

Before we continue the saga of the Federal Reserve and how it tinkers with the monetary system, let's discuss another very important economic concept: inflation.

10

★ ★ ★

INSIDIOUS INFLATION

When we see prices at the supermarket doubling or tripling, and yet government bean counters assure us that our inflation rate is running at a meager 2.1 percent, we're understandably perplexed. Something doesn't add up. We scratch our heads and wonder why we paid sixty thousand dollars this year for an automobile that cost only twenty thousand dollars two years ago. Then we discover that the house our uncle bought in the 1980s for a mere nineteen thousand dollars just sold for three hundred thousand dollars. We're convinced that inflation has hit with a vengeance, but the Consumer Price Index (CPI)—an inflationary indicator that measures changes in the prices urban consumers pay for "a representative basket of goods and services"[1]—insists that inflation in any given year hasn't increased over 3.4 percent since 1992. Now we're completely flummoxed. How can this be?

We *intuitively* know that something very odd is happening in our economy, but we can't quite put our finger on the problem. Contradictions abound everywhere. We see one thing but hear another. Government assurances ring hollow in the face of rising costs. Everyone seems to be anxiously waiting for the next shoe to drop, and we wonder how we can protect ourselves from impending disaster.

In this chapter we'll learn about inflation and its causes. *Hint:* tinkering with the monetary system is one of the culprits.

Kings and Coins

Most of us think of inflation as an increase in the overall price of goods and services. That's a very astute observation, but the definition is actually a bit more refined. In economic terms, *inflation* is "the *sustained increase* in the general level of *all* prices." In other words, the prices of all goods and services in the economy continue to rise over time, unless a major economic crisis forces the government to hit the reset button. In which case, the process begins all over again.

The phenomenon of inflation isn't anything new. Governments throughout history have tinkered with their monetary systems, racking up huge economic deficits and debt that have inevitably led to inflation or even hyperinflation. (*Note:* The *deficit* is a budgetary shortfall that happens when the government spends more than it collects in taxes and other revenue. The amount of money the government borrows to cover this budgetary deficit is the *national debt*).

As we discussed earlier, for a nation to have a functioning economy, it must produce goods and services to generate income and meet the needs of its people. But governments have enormous appetites, and when they want things they can't afford, it becomes an overwhelming temptation to tinker with the money supply.

Throughout history, the methods of tinkering with sovereign economies have been extremely creative. Early kings reserved the exclusive right to mint coins or print currency, which meant they had access to all the gold and silver coins that circulated through a kingdom's treasury. Of course, that access also gave kings free rein to tinker with the money supply.

When a king needed more money to bankroll his extravagant tastes, he simply had a portion of his kingdom's precious coins filed off or clipped. That was called *coin clipping.* Sometimes the coins were placed in a moistened leather bag, which was then shaken or beaten in a process called *coin sweating.* Fragments of the metal would fall off and cling to the inside of the bag. At other times, holes would be drilled through the coins to glean a portion of the precious metal. And on occasion, a king would mint coins using cheaper metal plated with gold or silver, thereby making a *coin sandwich*. Obviously, that would devalue (or debase) the coin.

After gleaning extra gold or silver from the old coins, the king then had new coins minted. Since he was the first to use the debased coins, he would pass them off at full value. Suddenly there were more coins in the money supply and fewer goods in the kingdom, since merchants were receiving less value for their products and couldn't afford to produce the same amount as before.

Merchants couldn't stop the king from playing his coin tricks, but they had a trick of their own up their sleeves. Since there was, let's say, 20 percent less gold in a clipped coin, merchants simply compensated by raising their prices 20 percent to offset the difference. Thus, the economy experienced a sustained increase in the general level of all prices—*inflation*!

What the king had cleverly done was to impose a 20 percent tax increase on the people without having to actually go out and collect it. Now he had the funds to purchase what he wanted.

Of course, it didn't take long for the king to realize that he now had a new problem. The people began using the debased coins to pay their regular taxes. He felt cheated, since he wasn't collecting as much gold as he once did. But no problem. Like a dog chasing his own tail, he simply repeated the whole operation.

Economist Adam Smith said that the kings who engaged in this practice

> were enabled, in appearance, to pay their debts and [fulfill] their engage-
> ments with a smaller quantity of silver [or gold] than would otherwise
> have been requisite. It was indeed in appearance only; *for their creditors*
> *were really defrauded* of a part of what was due to them. All other debtors
> in the state were allowed the same privilege, and might pay with the same
> nominal sum of the new and debased coin whatever they had borrowed in
> the old. Such operations … have always *proved favourable to the debtor, and*

ruinous to the creditor, and have sometimes produced a greater and more universal revolution in the fortunes of private persons, than could have been occasioned by a very great public calamity.[2]

Had the king confiscated his subjects' property or imposed a straight tax, it wouldn't have been nearly as harmful as inflation. A tax would have impacted only those who were taxed. But the tragedy of inflation is that it impacts *everyone* in a nation. The hard-earned money people have saved no longer has the value they thought it had. Creditors who loaned money anticipating a return are repaid with less value, and insurance values are wiped out.

England's superstar economist, John Maynard Keynes, once said,

There is no subtler, no surer means of overturning the existing basis of society than to debauch [devalue] the currency. The process engages all the hidden forces of economic law on the side of destruction, and does it in a manner which not one man in a million is able to diagnose.[3]

Kings and governments may think that tinkering with the money supply is the easiest way to replenish their empty coffers, but it sets in motion a host of destructive consequences.

Now that you know what inflation is, what do you think is the functional cause? See if you can identify it in the following little quiz.

Which of these statements is true?

a. Inflation is caused when companies are allowed to form monopolies and charge more for their products or services. OPEC (Organization of the Petroleum Exporting Companies) and cable companies are just a couple of examples.

b. Inflation is caused when products become scarce because of crop failures, strikes, or other factors that reduce supply.

c. The cause of inflation is an increase in the money supply in an economic system without a corresponding increase in goods or services.

d. Profiteering labor unions and business owners cause inflation because their greedy demands ultimately result in price increases.

Although price increases appear to be the root cause of inflation, they are, in reality, the *result* of inflation, not the cause. The correct answer is "c": the real cause of inflation is *an increase in the money supply without a corresponding increase in goods and services*. When new money is injected into the system without an equal increase in goods and services, the value of the money falls, and all prices rise. Had the king in our example been unable to alter the money supply, inflation would not have occurred.

Meat and Axes

We discovered in the previous section that inflation is *not* caused by *individual* producers raising their prices. It's caused by a sustained increase in the general level of *all prices across the board*, not just prices in one sector of the economy. So OPEC, trade unions, large companies, and individual merchants can raise their prices as high as they like, but it doesn't qualify as inflation until there's a *sustained* increase in *all* prices across *every* sector of the economy, without a *corresponding increase* in goods and services. Perhaps the following illustration will clarify:

One evening, Two-Toes Tom, Scarface-Salesman Sam, Wanda Wonder-Weaver, and Healthy-Hunter Harold were sitting by the campfire discussing an interesting proposition. Sam had just returned from visiting a faraway tribe in which everyone was involved in a new concept called *inflation*. All the tribe members had decided to double their prices so they would make twice the profit on their goods. What a great idea.

Our friends around the campfire agreed that it was high time their tribe adopted this practice as well. So they all rushed back to their tents to gather some of their own products to trade.

Healthy-Hunter Harold was beaming as he ran to his tent. *From now on,* he thought, *I'll only have to trade four packages of fresh meat for two stone axes instead of the usual eight. I can put twice as many trades together.*

Wanda Wonder-Weaver was also excited, since she would now be trading her blankets for twice as much. Two-Toes Tom, tired from working so hard, was glad that he could finally slow down a bit, since he would only have to produce half as many stone plows to trade for the same number of goods as before.

The four entrepreneurs returned to the campfire eager to get started with their trading. Healthy-Hunter Harold wanted to go first. Instead of the usual *eight* packages of fresh meat, he brought only *four* to trade with Sam for *two* stone axes, the usual number. But alas! Sam was standing there with only *one* axe, which he intended to trade with Harold for *eight* packages of meat. Sam argued that since inflation was *his* idea, he should be able to trade one axe for *eight* packages of meat. Harold said that would be fine, but the eight packages of meat would come off Sam's body.

By that time, it began to dawn on Wanda Wonder-Weaver that they couldn't cause inflation simply by raising their individual prices. It wouldn't make any difference how many people were involved or how many products were sold. *If one price went up, the other price must naturally come down.* And for inflation to occur, all prices had to increase across the board. Harold had raised his price by reducing the amount of meat he intended to trade for two of Sam's axes, which would have forced Sam to reduce his price. And Sam had raised his price by reducing the number of axes he planned to trade, expecting Harold to reduce his price for eight packs of meat. Wanda could see that wasn't going to work.

Our friends discovered that if one product goes up in price, then one, or a combination of other prices, must fall by precisely the same amount. Even if supply is scarce because of crop damage, labor strikes, or reductions from exports, the increase in the price paid for the scarce product will only result in less money with which to make other purchases.

For instance, if an oil cartel like OPEC raises the price of oil by $50 billion, there should be $50 billion less in the system for consumers to purchase other goods after they've paid extra at the gas pump. These other goods would then sit on the shelves collecting dust, which would cause a business *recession*, since other businesses would sell fewer products.

Wanda Wonder-Weaver sighed as she gathered her blankets and headed back to her tent. Two-Toes Tom returned to his tent and went to sleep, dreaming sadly of how close they had all come to becoming wealthy.

Hopefully you can see more clearly that regardless of the reasons individual prices are raised—scarcity, monopolies, greed, or wage demands—this does not *cause* inflation. There must be a sustained increase in the general level of *all prices*, without a *corresponding increase* in goods and services. As I mentioned earlier, price increases are a necessary *result* of inflation, not the cause.

Let's check in with our friends again and see if they've figured out how to create inflation.

Tents and Tiger Teeth

Scarface-Salesman Sam went to bed troubled. Why didn't *inflation* work in his tribe? What had he forgotten? Then he recalled that the other tribe wasn't using the barter system. They were using gold coins as a medium of exchange. Sam knew that his tribe had used tiger teeth as money before. So why wouldn't inflation work with tiger teeth just as well as with coins?

The next morning Sam rose early to explain his new idea to the others. First he told them they must stop using the barter system and start using tiger teeth as money. Then they must count the number of tiger teeth used as money and *double* that number so they could charge *twice* as much for the same number of products.

At that point Wanda Wonder-Weaver stopped weaving her blanket and laughed aloud. "With that kind of thinking," she said, "it's no wonder you guys are still primitive. Can't you see? Let's say you want to buy some tents. When you double the amount of money and the number of tents stays the same, it takes twice

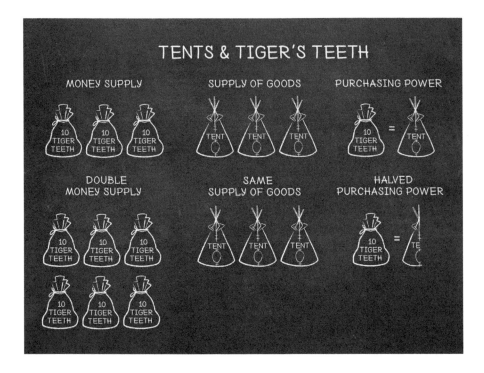

as much money to purchase the same number of tents. Your purchasing power is cut in half."

On the surface it might appear that the value of everything would increase in a scenario like this. But it doesn't. When there is a sustained increase in the general level of all prices, without a corresponding increase in goods and services, the only possible result is a *sustained decrease in the general value of the money supply*. In other words, if all prices rise at the same time, the money supply will fall in value at precisely the same time.

Let's say that all prices have risen across the board, and you go to the store to buy a gallon of milk. The *value* of that gallon of milk hasn't changed. You're still going to use the product as originally intended. But the value of your money has fallen, and you must now pay twice as much for that same precious gallon of milk. Your hard-earned money has just been stolen from you, and you had nothing to say about it.

Scarface-Salesman Sam misunderstood the concept of inflation because he misunderstood the *motive* behind the concept. All he observed was that the merchants in the other tribe were getting higher prices for their products, but he failed to see that inflation decreased the real value of the money (tiger teeth) they received. The chief of the other tribe was extracting a *silent tax* from his people in the form of inflation to pay off the debt for his last spending spree. Had the people realized what he was doing, they would have revolted. Ultimately, you can't play games with tents and tiger teeth.

MONETIZING THE DEBT— A MONETARY SLEIGHT OF HAND

N ow that we understand inflation a little better, let's return to our discussion of the Federal Reserve System. We learned previously that one of the ways the Fed alters the money supply is by turning the government's debt into spendable money. Let's take a closer look at how this monetary sleight of hand is accomplished.

As I mentioned earlier, the US Treasury Department deposits the money it collects from taxes, fees, and other charges in an account at a Federal Reserve Bank. From that account, checks are written to pay for every government expenditure. On occasion, however, the government encounters a very interesting dilemma: it spends more than it has in its account.

If your personal bank account were overdrawn, you would basically have two ways to resolve the problem: (1) earn enough money very quickly to cover the deficit, or (2) find someone who is willing to lend you the money.

Since the federal government doesn't earn money, it has only two alternatives to deal with the problem: (1) levy a new tax to raise more money, which falls under the government's *fiscal policy*, or (2) go to the marketplace to get a loan, which falls under the Federal Reserve's *monetary policy*. Either option is terribly hazardous to your health.

Dollars and Cherry Pies

In lieu of raising taxes, many less sophisticated countries would simply print new money to compensate for their overdrawn accounts and pay their debts. But the US government first opts to go to the marketplace for a loan. However, as we discussed earlier, the government can't borrow trillions of dollars from just one source. So it issues thousands of Treasury bills (T-bills), notes, and security bonds to US citizens and foreign countries. Selling bonds is sometimes referred to as the *bond illusion* because it gives the impression that the government has the ability and assets to cover its debts. But bonds, as well as T-bills and notes, are essentially IOUs the government promises to repay when the debts come due.

Let's say there are ten dollars and ten cherry pies in the system. The government wants one of the cherry pies but doesn't have the dollar to pay for it because its account is overdrawn. So it decides to offer a bond, figuring that one person in the system would rather own an interest-bearing bond than a cherry pie. So now there are ten dollars, ten cherry pies, and one bond in the system.

When it comes time to pay back the borrowed money *plus* the interest on the secured government bond, the Federal Open Market Committee of the Federal Reserve Bank calls in the bond (IOU) and pays it off. How does it do that? You guessed it ... *with newly created money.* In other words, "the Federal Reserve Banks, in paying for these securities, place *newly created reserves* in the accounts of the commercial banks at the Fed. (These reserves are created 'out of thin air,' so to speak.)" (emphasis added).[1]

The monetary sleight of hand takes place when a bond dealer—a middleman who handles the sale and redemption of bonds—purchases the bond from the owner and issues him a check. The bond dealer then delivers the bond to the Federal Reserve Bank in exchange for a check, which the bond dealer deposits in his bank account. The Federal Reserve Bank credits the deposited amount to the bank's reserves, and that bank is then entitled to make loans against that new reserve or exchange it for cash. But the Fed still holds the bond as an asset because it is still an

IOU signed by the US Treasury. In essence, what happens in the transaction is that the federal debt—a liability—is miraculously transformed into *an asset of spendable cash*. This is how the federal debt is monetized.

To illustrate, let's say that Barry Bond Dealer cashes in a bond with the Federal Reserve and receives a check for one thousand dollars in return. Barry then trots across town to his bank and deposits the check in his account. Since the Federal Reserve issued the check, the Fed credits the deposited amount to Barry's bank, and the bank's new reserves instantly rise by one thousand dollars. After holding one hundred dollars aside to satisfy the 10 percent fractional reserve requirement, Barry's bank now has nine hundred dollars' worth of newly created reserves. And voilà! The government has magically transformed its debt into spendable new money.

Monetizing the debt by using the intermediate step of issuing government bonds stalls the inflationary impact on the economy for at least a year, or perhaps much longer, depending on the term of the bond. If the government simply printed more money to pay its debts, the inflationary impact of adding newly created money to the system would be immediate.

Selling bonds, however, *ultimately* has exactly the same effect as if the government simply paid its debt with printing-press money or by entering ethereal numbers into a computer. Instead of having ten dollars and ten cherry pies and one bond in the system, there are now eleven dollars, ten cherry pies, and no bond (because the bond was cashed in).

The outcome is the same as the irresponsible actions of Germany when it paid war reparations after World War I. When forced to make the reparations, the Germans simply printed new German marks off their Fiat printing presses, and they were off the hook. That is until other countries started spending the money on German goods and services. With all that new money injected into the money supply, and with nothing to back it up, the value of the old marks plummeted, and the prices of all the German goods and services skyrocketed. The sustained increase in prices ultimately led to hyperinflation. Germans had to lug wheelbarrows full of German marks to the store to pay for just a few groceries. If a shopper was accosted on the way to the store, the thief would dump the worthless currency and steal the wheelbarrow.

When new money is injected into the money supply, it lowers the value of the money already in the system and causes a sustained increase in the general level of *all* prices. By now you know what that means—inflation.

When a government overdraws its account, selling bonds and T-bills may seem like a slick smoke-and-mirrors method for creating free money, but it isn't. On the contrary, it sets into motion silent but devastating consequences without Congress ever having to appeal to voters for tax increases.

What gave rise to the notion that the federal government could indulge its lust for overspending by taking out loans (selling bonds) and manufacturing new money? The answer to that question can be traced back to a very gloomy time in American history.

Boom, Bust, and Crash

Once upon a time, small clusters of sincere, hard-working people journeyed over treacherous seas to begin new lives in America. Their intentions were to carve out a peaceful and prosperous existence on a fabled piece of real estate that miraculously stretched all the way from the Atlantic Ocean to the Pacific Ocean. They dreamed of opportunities that would one day lead to prosperity, security, and happiness. Those dreams eventually became reality as their economic endeavors produced thousands of individual businesses that employed tens of thousands of their neighbors.

Their simple economy consisted of a system of bartering and a currency of metal coins and commodities, such as tobacco. By the late 1700s, the economy began to mature and even showed signs of sophistication. A business observer by the name of Jean-Baptiste Say wrote at the time that the very act of producing goods appeared to generate income equal to the value of the goods produced. That idea became known as *Say's Law*, which essentially states that *supply creates its own demand.* In other words, there will be sufficient spending to purchase all that is produced.

When times were good, business owners invested in capital goods and materials to build their enterprises. They would also buy raw materials to produce the items they wanted to sell. If they didn't have enough money of their own, they would invite investors to share in their business ventures. Through their hard work and diligence, their production efforts were successful. In fact, their endeavors often resulted in a surplus of goods that the marketplace couldn't absorb.

When a businessman's warehouse was full and the marketplace was saturated with his goods, he would have to lay off workers and halt production until the demand for his products increased and his warehouse emptied. Then he would start up his business again. On the downside, the lack of continuous production resulted in an economic *recession* that led to an increase in unemployment. That recurring business cycle became known as a *boom-and-bust cycle.*

Other observers in the late 1700s, including David Ricardo and Scottish economist James Mill, noticed these bumps in the business cycle, along with other interruptions, such as wars, gold rushes, and droughts. They concluded that over the long haul, the bumps tended to even out, production would resume, employment would recover, and demand would eventually equal supply. In time, spending would catch up with supply, and balance would be restored.

But some recessions were worse than others. During the seventy-five-year period in the United States prior to 1929, for example, there were *twenty-one* business recessions, with some gaps that lasted as long as two years.[2] Then came an economic recession so devastating that it became known as the Great Depression.

The Roaring Twenties had been a period of unprecedented easy money, credit abuse, speculation in risky ventures, and high expectations driven by greed and lack of fiscal discipline. But the stock-market crash in 1929 turned boom to bust in the blink of an eye. Panic ensued, and people converged on the banks en masse to withdraw their money. The banks, as we learned earlier, could never return all that money to their depositors at once. It had been loaned to borrowers who weren't expected to repay the money for ten or even twenty years. So when depositors realized they couldn't withdraw their money on demand, panic spread like wildfire to other depositors and banks.

It takes such a tiny pinprick to deflate the balloon of confidence in the banking system.

Early in the Great Depression, more than one-third of all US banks failed,[3] and depositors' funds evaporated into thin air, along with confidence in the system. More than twelve million people lost their jobs as unemployment catapulted past 20 percent. Industrial production dropped almost 50 percent, GDP plunged 30 percent, thousands of businesses failed, and per-capita income shrank. Hundreds of thousands of families lost their homes, and over half of home mortgages went into default.[4]

Local, county, state, and federal governments likewise panicked. They quickly increased taxes to cover their losses, but there was no money to pay the taxes. To make matters worse, the Federal Reserve Bank had failed miserably to protect depositors and restore confidence in the system by not moving money to the banks experiencing runs on their accounts. While the nation panicked and the banks floundered, the Fed did nothing. In fact, some Fed officials applauded the bank failures, insisting they were weeding out the weak banks and those with bad management practices.

Many believe that in the nation's hour of deepest need, when it was buckling under the relentless blows of the Great Depression, a savior named John Maynard Keynes came to the rescue. Conventional wisdom had failed—the "bumps" in the economic cycle had not evened out over time as promised. A new approach was needed, and Keynesian economics offered a promising solution.

Keynes' economic theory gave President Roosevelt and the US government all the justification it needed to spend, borrow, and manufacture money with the promise of restoring hope and prosperity to a devastated nation. Yet in spite of Keynes' brilliant ideas, the Depression droned on for more than ten miserable years, with no apparent end in sight.

Did Keynes' pet economic theory really save the day and lift the nation out of the Great Depression? When his theory was put to the test in the crucible of real life, were the results as glowing as its supporters would have us believe? Let's put Keynesian economics under the microscope and find out.

PART **2**

SYSTEMS MATTER

FROM THEORY
TO REALITY

N ow that we have a better grasp on some basic economic concepts, let's shift our focus to another important topic: economic and political systems. Earlier we asked why some countries are wealthy, while others are mired in poverty. A basic knowledge of economic concepts can offer some insight into this quandary, but if we really want to get to the heart of the issue, we need to focus on the role economic and political systems play in making nations and individuals better—or worse—off.

I'm continually amazed at how little the people of particular nations under-stand about the way their political and economic systems work or the factors that influence their individual choices and behaviors. In North Korea or Cuba, people get up at the crack of dawn, dress, and grab a bite to eat, and then climb into the back of a waiting truck that hauls them off to backbreaking work in rice paddies or pine-apple fields all day. In Taiwan, people sit in factories all day long next to conveyor belts and assemble very small parts for very big television sets. And in America, approximately eight million people don't even work at all.[1]

People all over the world go about their lives without ever stopping to ask why things are the way they are. They don't consider why they're expected to behave in certain ways. They just do it. They don't wonder why some economies function smoothly and others fail to function at all. They can't understand why some people have so much more of everything than others do—more wealth and abundance, more jobs, more resources, more goods and services, more opportunity, more health, more hope.

The average person on the street today may blame capitalism and free-market economics for a laundry list of earthly woes, including poverty, unemployment, and a lack of opportunity. But is that a fair assessment? Are capitalism and free enterprise truly the underlying causes of the suffering we see in so many parts of the world? Do some countries fare better economically than others merely because they have hoarded a larger slice of the pie? Wouldn't poverty be eliminated once and for all if we wiped out all market freedom and capitalistic institutions?

It can be tempting to arrive at such conclusions if we exclusively get our information from a marxist-leaning media. But as we'll discover in the following chapters, the fact that some countries are better off than others has comparatively little to do with greedy global corporations hogging all the wealth, and everything to do with the underlying economic and political systems those individual nations implement. As Dr. Paul Ballantyne, my graduate economics professor at the University of Colorado, used to proclaim, "Systems matter!"

The Laboratory of Real Life

We all know that the gap between theory and reality can be as wide as the Grand Canyon. Just as scientific theories must be subjected to rigorous testing by observation and experimentation to prove that their assertions are valid, economic theories must also be put to the test in the laboratory of real life to see whether their claims hold up.

When Isaac Newton arrived on the scene with a theory about gravity, the scientific community didn't immediately break out in a jig, declaring, "Eureka! He did it! Now we know why apples fall from trees." Newton's theory went through the same scrutiny and criticism every scientific theory must endure. Newton himself had lingering questions that his theory couldn't seem to answer, and it wasn't until centuries after his death that a genius by the name of Albert Einstein came along with his theory of relativity and effectively laid those questions to rest.

As I noted earlier, Say's Law of economics states that supply creates its own demand. This law passed muster in the nineteenth century but seemingly failed the litmus test during the Great Depression. John Maynard Keynes and other twentieth-century economists flatly rejected the assertion that the market would correct any imbalances. The proof, according to Keynes, was there for all to see: the Depression raged on, and the market had utterly failed to correct the imbalances or resolve the economic crisis. Thus, Say's Law was unceremoniously tossed on the trash heap with other debunked economic theories. But how did Keynes' pet economic theory fare when put to the test?

When Franklin D. Roosevelt implemented the New Deal in 1933, little did he know that the Great Depression would prove to be a perfect real-life laboratory for testing the validity of Keynes' theory. Keynes was convinced that his theory was the panacea for America's economic woes. If implemented as designed, he believed it would set the nation on the path to economic recovery and prosperity. It might even become the greatest economic system the world had ever known.

Peeking Behind the Curtain

Before we dissect Keynes' theory, let's talk about economic systems for a moment. Why do economic and political systems matter, and how do they impact our daily lives? How do they influence the way nations function? The better we understand systems, the easier it is to see why some nations enjoy abundance and others are stuck in an endless cycle of poverty.

Simply put, a *system* is "an organized body of beliefs, ideas, theories, principles, and practices." An economic system revolves around a distinct set of philosophical views, economic principles, and empirical practices. The principles and practices of an economic system ultimately determine the day-to-day decisions, management, and direction of an economy. When economic and political theories are put to the test as systems in the laboratory of real life, we soon discover whether those theories are valid. We can also discover by acute observation whether a particular system actually makes people better off. It's often been said, the proof is in the pudding.

We can readily see, for example, the unfortunate results of excessive taxation: companies may move to more business-friendly tax environments, outsource production and services to other countries, or curb capital expenditures and freeze hiring or lay off workers, which increases the unemployment rate. Fewer new businesses open their doors, and small businesses, crushed under an additional tax burden, may be forced out of business. Consumers hold on to their money rather than spending it and stimulating the economy. With more people out of work and struggling financially, services for the needy are often stretched beyond their resources, and crime, malnutrition, and poverty tend to increase. Not a pretty picture.

Economic hardship also compels people to seek government assistance, which increases dependency and reduces self-sufficiency, effectively draining resources rather than increasing revenue. In reality, a host of unintended negative consequences result from excessive taxation in spite of the theoretical benefits of pumping up government coffers to pay for more public services. Noteworthy examples of high-tax states are California, Oregon, Minnesota, New Jersey, and New York,[2] where in recent years, corporations and families have been leaving for greener pastures, unemployment and crime have been increasing, and people are increasingly dependent on government assistance.

By comparison, economic systems that promote low taxation encourage businesses to stay put and grow, spending money on capital investments and new hires, which decreases unemployment and, ironically, adds revenue to government coffers. More people working means even more tax revenue and consumer spending, which results in greater economic growth. Less strain and drain on public and private resources also means that those who are struggling financially can find the help they need to get back on their feet. Obstacles are removed for new businesses to blossom and grow. More funding is available to control crime and address other problems. States like Alaska, Texas, Nevada, and Wyoming have been reaping the economic benefits of low taxes for years.[3]

The economic policies and practices in each example and the real-life results reflect the underlying economic systems the respective governments adopted and implemented. The contrast is stunning, isn't it? That's why systems matter.

If we peek behind the curtain to discover why things are the way they are, we'll usually find that the "wizards" who are calling the shots favor particular economic and political systems. Those systems not only influence events at national, state, and local levels, but they also have a direct impact on our individual behaviors and choices. By seeking to understand the philosophical views at the heart of each system, we can learn to assess the real-life results and evaluate whether a system is actually making people better off.

Utopian theories often sound appealing, equitable, and compassionate, but in practice they can be disastrous for everyone except the wizards calling the shots. Just as actions speak louder than words, results speak louder than empty promises.

Every society eventually develops a political and economic system. Some systems are rooted in sound, defensible philosophies; others are nothing but a hodge-podge of trial and error that morphs into a system by default. Still other systems are based on the ideological views of strong, charismatic leaders who inspire people's trust and loyalty.

Practically speaking, economic systems are necessary to determine what goods are produced and who owns them, how they are produced and distributed, who ends up with them, and what they cost. Economic systems must also figure out how to manage change and promote technological progress.

Political and economic systems are generally divided into two polar extremes: the *command system* and the *free-market system*. The command system is based on a redistributive model in which wealth is taken from the producers and distributed as the command structure sees fit. Marxism, socialism, and communism are examples of a command or redistribution system. The free-market or growth system, on the other hand, is based on freedom of individual economic and cultural choice. Capitalism and the free-market, or free-enterprise, system fall into this category.

As we'll see in the following chapters, these two competing systems dominate the world stage today. They approach wealth and poverty from opposite ends of the philosophical spectrum and deliver very different results. But before we explore the origins and aspects of these polar extremes, let's finish our discussion of Keynesian economics and the transformative role it played during the Great Depression. Keynes firmly believed that his economic theory would save the day, but did it deliver as promised?

BATHTUB ECONOMICS

From the ivy-covered cloisters of Harvard, Yale, and Princeton to the nondescript classrooms of obscure community colleges, John Maynard Keynes is revered today as the brilliant economist from King's College in Cambridge, England, who saved the United States and the world from the Great Depression. Whenever his name is mentioned, all jokes about nerdy economists in wire-rimmed glasses cease, and a sacred hush falls over the room.

As the legend goes, Keynes published the body of his exalted teachings in *The General Theory of Employment, Interest, and Money* in 1936, and the newly elected US president, Franklin D. Roosevelt, stumbled across the book in the nick of time. FDR read the magic words—which advocated government deficit spending during recessionary cycles to bolster employment—and meticulously implemented every jot and tittle. The president's timely actions miraculously transformed an impoverished nation into an economic superpower, the likes of which the world had never seen.

One of the glaring problems with this legend is that FDR engineered the first New Deal following his 1932 election victory, but Keynes' book wasn't published until 1936. Another uncomfortable truth is that none of the Keynes-Roosevelt shenanigans actually lifted the nation out of the Great Depression.

Bathtub Economics in a Nutshell

So what were the exalted teachings of Mr. Keynes?

Dr. Paul Ballantyne once told me, "Jim, if you want to easily remember the economic philosophy of John Maynard Keynes, just visualize a bathtub about one-third full of water. Above the tub is a spigot with a handle to regulate the inflow of water. Above the spigot are the letters *G* and *I*, which stand for *Government* and *Investment*. As with all bathtubs, there is a drain at the bottom of the tub. Over the drain are the letters *T* and *S*, which stand for *Taxes* and *Savings*.

"If you want to pump up and regulate the economy, you simply turn on the spigot and plug up the drain pipe. By increasing *government spending* and *investment* while preventing *taxes* and *savings* from draining out of the economy, you can presumably increase the level of income and reduce unemployment."

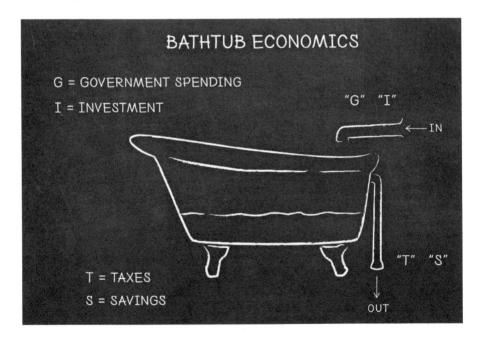

"But what's so brilliant or novel about that?" I asked. "In 1913, the Federal Reserve was empowered to tinker with the money supply by raising or lowering reserve percentages and lending rates, as well as monetizing the federal debt by selling and buying back notes and security bonds. What's new about Keynes?"

Keynes had witnessed firsthand the depression and high unemployment Great Britain suffered through after the First World War. He had also carefully observed the series of recessions across the pond in the United States, as well as the early years of the Great Depression from 1929 through 1935. Based on those observations, he was convinced that the severe bumps of the boom-and-bust economic cycles could be flattened out with his *"aggregate demand" expenditures model*. He argued that Say's Law and other economic theories simply weren't dependable. The Great Depression supplied all the necessary proof. If the economy was left to correct itself, it would never happen. Government intervention was required to smooth out the bumps in the cycle.

Keynes believed it was the government's responsibility to control the national economy, ensure stability, and play an active role in economic policies and procedures. The esteemed economist was also a strong advocate of government ownership of utilities and transportation and control over housing.

Keynesian economic theory was touted as the solution to the age-old problems of recessionary market cycles, economic depressions, and unemployment. Bathtub economics essentially promised prosperity through profligate government spending—a ridiculous and illogical claim that amazingly caught traction in an atmosphere of desperation and has yet to lose its appeal. Many sing the praises of bathtub economics, but what about the pitfalls?

The Slippery Flaws of Bathtub Economics

You may recall this insightful statement from John Maynard Keynes:

There is no subtler, no surer means of overturning the existing basis of society than to debauch the currency. The process engages all the hidden forces of economic law on the side of destruction, and does it in a manner which not one man in a million is able to diagnose.[1]

Keynes was absolutely right. Debauch the currency, and you destroy the integrity of the economic system. At that point, the very fabric of society begins to unravel. And yet the process is so silent and so subtle that people don't comprehend what's happening. In my work with Project C.U.R.E., I've witnessed this firsthand in a number of developing countries.

In 1986, while I was in Brazil working with President Sarney and one of his chief economists on Brazil's debt repayment to US banks, the country was experiencing 3,000 percent inflation. I would watch women line up outside factory fences waiting for their husbands to get paid at the end of each afternoon shift. The husbands would emerge from the factory, run to the fence, and hand their pay to their wives. The wives would then run to the market and buy whatever was available, because the next day the prices would double or triple. As Keynes so astutely observed, debauching the currency ignites economic and cultural chaos.

The most frightening aspect of Keynes' statement is that it can reflect either a passive observation or an active strategy. In other words, it can *passively* explain what happens to a culture whose currency has been debauched, or it can be used as an active strategy to destroy a targeted economy and culture.

Aside from debauching the currency, which I'd say is a pretty glaring defect, bathtub economics has a few other slippery flaws:

1. *Balanced budgets aren't a priority.* In fact, balancing the budget isn't even a serious consideration in bathtub economics. The idea, after all, is to spend your way to prosperity. Spend as if you're rich, and it will become a self-fulfilling prophecy.

Do I even have to point out the flaws in that logic? If you follow this theory to its natural conclusion, you'll discover in the end that it will land you in a mess of trouble. Anyone who spends more than he has finds out soon enough that he has spent his way to poverty.

2. *Government is viewed as the true source of wealth and unending supply.* The only way government could ever be considered the true source of wealth is if it never runs out of citizens to tax. Remember, government has only two alternatives for generating income: raising taxes or borrowing money. That should give us a pretty clear idea where all the wealth comes from. To paraphrase Margaret Thatcher, the trouble with bathtub economics is that you eventually run out of other people's money.

3. *The bathtub-economics model offers no way to measure the real rate of inflation.* It's impossible to know what's happening with the true value of our money because it doesn't really matter. But as we learned earlier, arbitrarily increasing the money supply without increasing the products or services in the system simply devalues the currency and forces *all prices* to go up. Remember: inflation is a sustained increase in the general level of all prices. Since bathtub economists don't worry about trifling things like the value of your money, they simply tweak the inflation indicators to make it look like inflation is under control.

As I mentioned earlier, inflation has historically been measured by the Consumer Price Index (CPI), in which the Feds cherry-pick a market basket of items and track the prices for a specified period. If the prices go up by 9 percent during this period, then the recorded inflation rate increases by 9 percent. But in the 1980s and 1990s, people reacted negatively to the high rate of inflation. They empirically knew that the prices they were paying were doubling even though they were assured that the CPI was targeted at 2 percent inflation. So the Fed tinkered with the yard stick by changing the items in the market basket that are tracked for price increases.[2] All the government had to do was pull the expensive items—like food, utilities, and housing—out of the market basket and replace them with cheap imported goods like two-dollar shirts from Hong Kong and one-dollar socks from China. The CPI prices then complied with the targeted percentages. No problem.

On January 25, 2012, the Federal Reserve took the tinkering one step further by announcing that it would start using the personal consumption expenditures

(PCE) price index to track inflation and would set a new inflation target.[3] The Federal Reserve Open Market Committee (FOMC) now arbitrarily implements a monetary policy that will "maintain an inflation rate of 2 percent over the medium term."[4] But the problem hasn't been solved. There's still an ugly gorilla in the room. How long can the government continue to hide or ignore seventeen trillion dollars of monetized debt from unrestrained deficit spending without admitting to hyperinflation? What pinprick will finally pop the balloon of confidence in our economic system?

4. *Keeping the bathtub full is unrealistic and impossible over the long term.* Once a government embarks on the path of deficit spending, it gets harder and harder to find justifiable ways to keep the bathtub full. Massive projects are needed to keep up the colossal deficit spending. FDR's administration spent obscene amounts of money on government programs and agencies. Joseph Kennedy was very effective raising campaign funds for the Roosevelt elections, but when his son John Fitzgerald became president, an even larger challenge emerged: keeping the bathtub full. What worthy project did JFK come up with? NASA, of course. The United States simply had to beat the Ruskies to the moon, and we outspent them to do it.

Bathtub fillers during the Johnson administration included the War on Poverty and Lady Bird's bottomless expense account to beautify America. Jimmy Carter and the Clintons, as well as the Bushes, almost lost the bathtub with spending programs and economic-stimulus packages, even in the final hours of George W. Bush's presidency.

Each occasion of filling the bathtub with deficit spending requires a larger and more complicated government program until the tub overflows and floods the entire house.

The problem with all that spending is that in the end it doesn't solve the problems it promises to fix. Why? Because functioning economies must *produce* something tangible and of value to people. In the end, deficit spending accomplishes nothing but digging a deeper hole and then paying someone else to fill it back up.

BATHTUB ECONOMICS
AND THE NEW DEAL

W hile John Maynard Keynes was refining his bathtub economics theory across the big pond, the Great Depression raged on in the United States. For three years the country had been traumatized by the worst economic crisis imaginable, and most of the world's economies were embroiled in the international scramble over gold supplies and debt repayments.

Herbert Hoover was president in 1929 when the stock market crashed and the nation spiraled downward into gloom and despair. But in 1932, Franklin Delano Roosevelt appeared on the scene as a new voice of hope. The charismatic governor of the state of New York challenged Hoover for the presidency, garnering 57 percent of the popular vote and nearly 90 percent of electoral vote.[1]

The irony of Roosevelt's election campaign is worth a short review at this point.

Changing Horses Midstream

During the 1932 campaign, Roosevelt reiterated the old-line party speeches, promising to reduce all public expenditures, do away with useless government commissions and offices, consolidate federal departments and bureaus, and eliminate government extravagances. He even promised to balance the budget.

FDR castigated Hoover for running huge deficits and roundly chastised him for his inability to halt the effects of the Depression or restore any semblance of prosperity. At one point in the campaign, Roosevelt even stated, "Our industrial plant is built; the problem just now is whether under existing conditions it is not overbuilt. Our last frontier has long since been reached."[2]

Ironic words compared to the radical economic policies FDR set in motion following the election. It almost seems as if Roosevelt and Hoover switched their campaign promises.

What caused Roosevelt to reverse course so abruptly?

Without a doubt, the cultural and economic changes taking place at the time had a significant influence on the newly elected president. By the early 1930s, the intellectual atmosphere on university campuses around the world had undergone a fundamental shift toward liberal progressivism. The US presidency, which had been dominated by Republicans till 1932, now began a decades-long trend toward Democratic candidates.

The economic and cultural pendulums, nationally and internationally, were also swinging away from individual responsibility and a decentralized, limited government to social outcome equality and a powerful centralized government. Proponents of a centralized system called for the federal government to control the economy and protect citizens from misfortune, even if that meant government ownership and operation of the means of production. John Maynard Keynes and his comrades were on the front lines leading the charge.

Behind Closed Doors

Between the 1932 election and FDR's inauguration the following March, the president-elect huddled with an elite group of intellectuals—the Brain Trust—at the governor's mansion in Albany, New York, to forge a strategy for his first term in office. From that meeting emerged FDR's New Deal.

We'll never know exactly what took place at that fateful meeting, but had a little mouse been watching from his lofty perch on a bookcase, he just might have overhead a professor explaining the new theory of a prominent British economist.

"You see," remarked the professor, "running an economy is like adjusting the water level in a bathtub. As long as the government keeps the bathtub full, we can spend our way to prosperity and lift ourselves out of the Depression." He even drew a diagram to illustrate his point.

One member of the group asked where all the money for the government spending would come from. The professor insisted it didn't make any difference.

Other members raised equally challenging questions, but Johnny One Note just kept giving the same answer: "It doesn't matter. Just keep the bathtub full."

Up to that point in the discussion, the newly elected president hadn't said a word. He just sat there staring at the cartoonish bathtub drawing. Then the hint of a smile began to play at the corners of his mouth, and moments later he broke out in a grin. The bathtub economics theory wasn't so much an economic model as it was a political model. It was a "new deal".

FDR had just been afforded an irresistible opportunity to fundamentally transform the nation and perhaps even change the very nature of democracy. But fundamental change wouldn't happen overnight. He needed to ensure that he would be in office for a long, long time.

Accomplishing this grand vision would require solid voting blocks from every demographic group in America. The future president wasn't really concerned about how the boom-and-bust business cycles could be worked out. He saw the magic of turning deficit spending into real money that could be used to buy votes and foster dependency on government. If he could get 50 percent of the voters on board with his New Deal, they would become dependent on his subsidies and continue voting him into office. With a solid block of voters, he could secure control over the economy and the political machinery of the nation—and radically transform the cultural-economic system. All he had to do was keep the bathtub full.

Only that little mouse knows the real story, but the New Deal that emerged from this presidential powwow seemed to fit Keynes' bathtub economics theory to a T.

Bathtub Economics in Action

Behind those closed doors in Albany, a philosophical coalition took shape. The Brain Trust was convinced that the Depression was a failure of capitalism, and active intervention on the part of a centralized government was the appropriate remedy. Relief, recovery, and reform would be the core themes of Roosevelt's economic strategy for the next four years.

On March 4, 1933, Roosevelt was fired up as he delivered his inaugural address. He blamed the stock-market crash, the Depression, and the economic crisis on the greed and self-interest of capitalism and castigated bankers and financiers for their quest for profit:

> Practices of the unscrupulous money changers stand indicted in the court of public opinion. … [They] have fled from their high seats in the temple of our civilization. We may now restore that temple to the ancient truths. The measure of the restoration lies in the extent to which we apply social values more noble than mere monetary profit.[3]

Roosevelt never once admitted that the US government and the inaction of the Fed were also to blame for the crisis.

One of the first actions the new president took was to declare a bank holiday.[4] All US banks were closed from March 6 through March 9 and reopened only after Congress passed the Emergency Banking Act. The Federal Deposit Insurance Corporation (FDIC) bill soon followed. Convenience and confidence in the system had to be restored. Depositors would no longer have to depend on bank reliability but could trust the government to protect their deposits. "The only thing we have to fear is fear itself,"[5] Roosevelt proclaimed as he laid out his bold recovery plan.

The New Deal, as Roosevelt called it, was the remedy that would bring the nation back from the brink of economic disaster and despair. During FDR's first one hundred days in office, a record number of bills was sent to Congress for approval at a special emergency session. Soon there were so many relief, recovery, and reform bills moving through Congress, it was hard to keep track of them. Any government programs that failed to pass or were held up for some reason were reinstituted by executive order. Congress then had to override the orders, or the Supreme Court had to strike them down as unconstitutional.

During his second term, Roosevelt proposed a shocking law that would allow him to appoint up to six new Supreme Court justices so that he could have a "persistent infusion of new blood."[6] Even his own vice president protested, claiming that the president was violating the separation of powers, and that such a law would give him absolute control over the Supreme Court by means of *court packing.* Over time, however, Roosevelt eventually got his "infusion of new blood," appointing to the court eight of nine justices, who ratified his policies with ease.

FDR's New Deal, also brought about an explosion in the size and scope of government beyond what anyone could have envisioned. And it opened the floodgates for government bureaucracy to spread its tentacles throughout every sector of the economy and society. Thanks to the New Deal, the concept of limited government, as America's founders envisioned it, was purged from the scene, replaced by a dizzying array of federal agencies—aptly nicknamed the Alphabet Agencies. Among them were:

- the Federal Communications Commission (FCC)
- the Federal Housing Administration (FHA)
- the National Labor Relations Board (NLRB)
- the Securities and Exchange Commission (SEC)
- the Social Security Administration (SSA)
- the Tennessee Valley Authority (TVA).

In true Keynesian fashion, FDR's government wasted no time seizing control over the economy, industry, labor, utilities, housing, and anything else it could get its hands on.

It's also interesting to note that the New Deal programs shared some eerie similarities with the 1928 Socialist Party platform, including national ownership of natural resources, transportation, communication, and utilities; national unemployment insurance and old-age pensions; a system of national health insurance; and increased taxes for high-income earners, corporations, and inheritance.

Keynes had insisted that recessions and depressions wouldn't correct themselves but required government intervention and unbridled economic control. Such authoritative declarations proffered by a renowned economist effectively sanctioned the actions FDR and his cast of political cronies wanted to pursue in the first place. In turn, FDR and his New Deal elevated Keynes to almost godlike status and gave his economic theories added credence. Roosevelt needed Keynes, and Keynes needed Roosevelt.

A Revealing Glimpse into Keynes and FDR

For years the relationship between FDR and Keynes was left to conjecture. But in recent years, correspondence has surfaced that reveals the influence of Keynes and his economic theories on Roosevelt. As I've studied these letters more closely, I'm surprised that the United States didn't travel further and more quickly down the road to progressive socialism than it did.

Politics and economics make strange bedfellows, and the relationship between Keynes and FDR is a prime example. We can't fully appreciate Roosevelt's actions in radically transforming America and redefining the structure, role, and reach of government unless we understand his relationship with John Maynard Keynes.

Keynes saw himself not just as an economist and author but as Roosevelt's mentor and adviser, guiding him through the economic and social changes he was implementing in America through the New Deal. Keynes progressively increased pressure on FDR to move America more quickly toward a centralized, government-controlled economic system. In December of 1933, Keynes published an open letter to the president in the *New York Times*, using the bully pulpit to spur Roosevelt to action. "Dear Mr. President," Keynes wrote,

You have made yourself the Trustee for those in every country who seek to mend the evils of our condition by reasoned experiment within the framework of the existing social system. If you fail, rational change will be gravely prejudiced throughout the world, leaving orthodoxy and revolution to fight it out. But if you succeed, new and bolder methods will be tried everywhere, and we may date the first chapter of a new economic era from your accession to office. …

You are engaged on a double task, Recovery and Reform—recovery from the slump and the passage of those business and social reforms which are long overdue. For the first, speed and quick results are essential. The second may be urgent too; but haste will be injurious, and wisdom of long-range purpose is more necessary than immediate achievement. [Your] success in short-range Recovery … will [give you] the driving force to accomplish long-range Reform.[7]

Keynes went on to lecture his pupil on the "fallacies" of FDR's implementation of the New Deal, and then dictated the steps necessary for a course correction. It sounded as if Keynes was afraid that FDR wouldn't implement Keynes' grand Socialist agenda quickly and thoroughly enough to save the United States and the world. It seems to me that Keynes saw himself as an economic maestro who was afraid that his pupil wouldn't quite get the scope and importance of the performance and would mess up the whole concert, thereby depriving the maestro his deserved place in history.

Later, in 1938, Keynes penned a private letter to Roosevelt expressing grave concern that the president would jeopardize the progressive cause by not taking the Keynesian game plan seriously enough:

When I was with you [Roosevelt] three and a half years ago the necessity for effective new [housing] measures was evident. … But what happened? Next to nothing. … I should advise putting most of your eggs in this basket [and] making absolutely sure that they are being hatched without delay. … If a direct subsidy is required to get a move on …, it should be given without delay or hesitation. … I [also] think there is a great deal to be said for the ownership of all the utilities by publicly owned boards. …

[Your] position [on the railroads] seems to be exactly what it was three or four years ago. … Nationalize them if the time is ripe. …

You [can] do anything you [like] with [businessmen], if you … treat them (even the big ones) … as domestic animals by nature, even though they have been badly brought up and not trained as you would wish. …

I accept the view that durable investment must come increasingly under state direction. … I regard the growth of collective bargaining as essential. I approve minimum wage and hours regulation. … But I am terrified lest progressive causes in all the democratic countries should suffer injury, because you have taken too lightly the risk to their prestige which would result from a failure measured in terms of immediate prosperity. There need be no failure.[8]

What lucid examples of transformation taking place at the intersection of culture and economics.

The strange saga of Roosevelt and Keynes transforms into a classic tragedy as the true nature of their relationship becomes clear. Each character became increasingly codependent on the other to fulfill his personal dreams and ambitions. Roosevelt was willing and eager to keep Keynes' bathtub of deficit spending full to secure his place in history as the world's preeminent political leader and supplier of free goodies that would buy him the votes to stay in power. And Keynes saw his opportunity to use Roosevelt's unique political position and the crisis of the Great Depression to establish his legacy as the most influential evangelist for the economic philosophies of Marx, Engels, and Lenin.

The Magic Pill?

Was bathtub economics the magic pill that lifted America out of the Great Depression? Should John Maynard Keynes and FDR get the credit for saving the United States from economic disaster? What indeed were the results of the New Deal and Keynesian economic policies?

I would argue that all of the tinkering with aggregate expenditures ultimately had very little to do with delivering the United States from the iron grip of the Depression. If anything, Keynesian economics prolonged the agony. And yet many today view Keynes as some kind of god who saved the world. It's still politically correct to grab a sign and march for the liberal-progressive agenda of spending our way out of bankruptcy. In recent years Keynesian economics has seen a resurgence among economists who embrace Keynes' belief that business cycles should be managed by the government.[9] But is all the godlike reverence for Keynes justified?

The time-tested formula for economic success is indisputable. Functioning economies are built on production. They must produce goods and services to generate income. When production runs so smoothly and efficiently that warehouse shelves become jam-packed with goods and the market can't sell enough to keep pace, production has to stop until sales catch up. That's when Barney Businessman sends his workers home until demand for his product increases, and he needs to crank the machinery back up to start producing more goods. As we learned earlier, economists call this the boom-and-bust cycle of business.

One gaggle of economists would advise Barney not to stock up on so much material or hire so many workers all at once, since getting the job done too fast and efficiently will only result in a surplus of goods and laying off his workers. "Pace yourself," they'd tell him. "Stretch out the gaps, and the economy will run more smoothly."

Keynes and his gaggle of bathtub economists, on the other hand, would tell Barney that the simple ups and downs of the business cycle won't work themselves out. "Don't slow down," they'd advise him. "If you cut back on workers and material, that will seriously reduce output and result in massive unemployment. You have to keep the spending up and the bathtub full."

Keynesian economists cling to the belief that a country can spend its way out of economic trouble. Government control and deficit spending will supposedly smooth out the bumps in the boom-and-bust cycle, effectively reduce unemployment, and lead to prosperity. Many believe this formula was the magic pill that eventually ended the Depression. They insist that the Depression would have lasted far longer had it not been for Keynes and FDR's New Deal.

An interesting argument, but the evidence is clear that years of government tinkering with the monetary system did remarkably little to end the Depression. Despite a full bathtub, unemployment persisted, and the economy continued to languish. In truth, the economy didn't turn around until the United States was drawn into World War II. That was when the rusty wheels of production began to turn once again. During the military buildup for war, factories began hiring workers to produce essential goods, unemployment began to drop, and incomes began to rise. Ever so slowly the ship turned around, and prosperity was restored. But World War II was a horrible price to pay to end the Great Depression.

Bathtub economics wasn't the magic pill it purported to be. As is so often the case, theories look a whole lot different in the glaring light of reality.

POLES APART

The previous chapters gave us a glimpse into why economic and political systems matter, but we'll need to travel a bit further back in history to understand the systems that are competing for dominance in the world today. Our journey begins across the pond in Great Britain.

The Free-Enterprise Evangelist

We've already noted the inspirational and philosophical role the Magna Carta played in shaping the great American experiment of 1776. This magnificent "Charter of Freedom" loomed large in the minds of America's founders as they forged a new nation from the bedrock principle that all human beings have been "endowed by their Creator with … unalienable rights [to] Life, Liberty, and the pursuit of Happiness."[1] The vision set forth in the Magna Carta, which limited government power and guaranteed rights and liberty for the people, echoed in every word of America's founding documents.

America was built upon this "cornerstone of liberty"—as the Magna Carta has been called—but we can't ignore another essential influence that shaped this free and prosperous nation.

On March 9, 1776, Scottish economist Adam Smith published a groundbreaking economic work titled *An Inquiry into the Nature and Causes of the Wealth of Nations*. Smith had grown up in an agrarian mercantile culture that functioned under the watchful eye of the British monarchy. But Smith and his generation had also enjoyed significant advantages afforded by the Magna Carta. Smith himself was a brilliant professor of economics who had an insatiable curiosity about the world and how it worked. I like to think of him as the world's first cultural economist because he was interested in people as well as economics.

Smith was particularly intrigued with the differences between rich and poor countries and why those differences existed. His curiosity compelled him to leave his university position and become a traveling tutor so he could research various economic and political systems.[2] Based on his observations, Smith identified several key factors that characterized successful economic systems. He later recorded his conclusions in *The Wealth of Nations*, as his book is commonly referred to, and thus became known as the father of modern economics.

According to Smith, the role of government is

first ... protecting the society from the violence and invasion of other independent societies; ... secondly ... protecting, as far as possible, every member of the society from the injustice or oppression of every other member of it, or the duty of establishing an exact administration of justice; ... and, thirdly ... erecting and maintaining certain public works and certain public institutions, ... [since] the profit could never repay the expense to any individual, or small number of individuals.[3]

In nations that were better off, Smith observed that the functions of government were essentially limited to protecting citizens from foreign and domestic threats and maintaining certain public works that individuals were unable to offer.

Smith emphasized that governments should not interfere with economic competition or free trade, which, he believed, were necessary for strong economic growth. Like Thomas Jefferson, Adam Smith viewed centralized government power as a great danger to ordinary citizens, and concluded that the people needed protection from government tyranny.

As he considered the question of wealth and poverty, Smith came to the conclusion that apart from the "natural course of things," the only other necessary factors for a nation trapped in poverty to become better off are peace, limited taxation, and the right to enjoy the fruits of one's labor. Smith further asserted that "the natural effort of every individual to better his own condition, when [allowed] to exert itself with freedom and security, is so powerful a principle, that it is alone, and without any assistance … capable of carrying on the society to wealth and prosperity."[4]

Wealth, as Smith defined it, refers to the "annual produce of the land and labour of the society."[5] In other words, *the ability to produce income determines the true wealth of any nation.* Smith observed that wealthy nations generated more income, and poor nations generated less.

What enabled a nation to generate more income? Smith concluded through research and firsthand observation that the key to increasing income is an economic system based on individual freedom.

"The progress of our North American and West Indian colonies," he stated, "would have been much less rapid, had no capital but what belonged to themselves been employed in exporting their surplus produce"[6] By means of free trade, poorer countries were able to trade their raw products for manufactured luxuries of wealthier countries. "Thus the wool of England used to be exchanged for the wines of France, and the fine cloths of Flanders, in the same manner as the corn of Poland is … exchanged for the wines and brandies of France, and for the silks and velvets of France and Italy."[7]

The principles of capitalism and free enterprise were essential to wealth creation, Smith argued, whereas restrictive and oppressive economic systems appeared to magnify poverty.

Smith also noted that self-interest—a primal, psychological human drive—could be harnessed for the benefit of society instead of degenerating into selfishness. (We'll discuss this criticism of free enterprise in a later chapter.) His concept of a free-enterprise system ignited the great experiment of 1776 and fueled the hopes and dreams of becoming better off for generations to come.

The Evangelist of Communism

Approximately one hundred years after Adam Smith wrote his seminal work, *The Wealth of Nations*, along came German philosopher and economist Karl Marx. A proponent of communism, Marx wrote perhaps the most influential economic work of the nineteenth century, *Das Kapital*.

Like Smith, Marx was a product of his time. Born in the Prussian Rhineland in 1818, Marx was Jewish, but his father had converted to Christianity before Marx was born. Baptized in the Lutheran Church as a child, Marx would later embrace atheism.

In 1835, at the age of seventeen, Marx enrolled at the University of Bonn in Germany, where he joined the Trier Tavern Club (a drinking society). As a student he became embroiled in serious disputes and even ended up in a duel. Marx seemed to believe that his role in life was to challenge ideas he viewed as illusions, errors, or deceptions. But his rebellious lifestyle and controversial views often stirred up conflict.

In 1842, Marx became a contributor and editor for a liberal newspaper in Cologne, Germany. After marrying his long-time fiancée, Jenny von Westphalen, the two moved to Paris, where Marx joined a group of French radicals and eventually met Friedrich Engels, who became a lifelong friend and colleague. While in Paris, Marx began calling for the proletariat (working class) to rise up against the bourgeoisie (the ruling class), and his radical views eventually led to his expulsion from France.

In the spring of 1845, Engels followed Marx to Belgium, where they collaborated on several writing projects. The two men eventually returned to Paris, where they published their definitive work *The Communist Manifesto* in 1848. The following year, Marx was deported from France yet again and moved to London with his family.

In 1867, Marx penned *Das Kapital*, taking issue with Adam Smith's views and arguing that the only solution to the struggle between the classes was for the masses to rise up against the oppressive exploitation of the bourgeoisie, which included employers and property owners.

In *The Communist Manifesto*, Marx expressed utter disdain for free-market capitalism:

> The bourgeoisie … has pitilessly torn asunder the motley feudal ties that bound man to his "natural superiors," and has left remaining no other nexus between man and man than naked self-interest. … It has resolved personal worth into exchange value, and in place of the numberless indefeasible chartered freedoms, has set up that single, unconscionable freedom— Free Trade. … [And it has substituted] naked, shameless, direct, brutal exploitation.[8]

Marx believed that the free-enterprise system was the cause of interpersonal strife, income inequality, and poverty and must therefore be abolished. The Communist system, by contrast, would restore and ensure peace, equality, and prosperity. Indeed, Marx fully expected that one day the masses would see the inherent flaws of the free-enterprise system and overthrow it. In its place, they would demand the communistic ideals of equality and wealth redistribution.

Naturally, under the Communist system, private ownership would be eliminated. No wealth, property, or inheritance would be owned by any single individual. The "means of production" would be distributed (or redistributed) to everyone equally—"from each according to his ability, to each according to his needs."[9] (This view, of course, also reflects the philosophy of socialism.) All sectors of the economy and society would be controlled and maintained by the state, including banking, transportation, utilities, housing, communication, education, and industry.

Even though the masses were assured that they would govern themselves, there was never any question in Marx's mind that an elite group of intellectuals— the politburo—would need to exercise total control. The class struggle necessarily leads to the "dictatorship of the proletariat,"[10] Marx wrote. Apparently the masses, who were wise enough to throw off the fetters of an unjust, oppressive, capitalistic government, could not be trusted to govern themselves under communism.

As a Communist, Marx also had a disdain for religion and considered it "the opium of the people." Although he was often quite hostile in his rhetoric, Marx believed that once the working class freed itself from the false constraints of religion, it would become irrelevant and fade away.[11] Indeed, the Communist system is incompatible with religion, since communism is inherently humanistic, exalting human reason and the power of the state.

To the end, Marx believed that the greed and self-interest embodied in capitalism and free enterprise were the main cause of poverty and misery in the world. Marx himself spent the rest of his days unemployed and living in abject poverty with his family in London. To survive, he relied on a meager inheritance and the financial support of his friend Friedrich Engels.

For Marx and the downtrodden masses, Marxism and the Communist system offered the only hope of equality and prosperity. But the masses never rose up to overthrow the greedy bourgeoisie, and Marx perished waiting for his worldwide revolution.

Marx's Protégé

We need to add one more character to this intriguing saga of economic and political systems: Vladimir Ilyich Ulyanov, aka Vladimir Lenin. Lenin is best known as the founder of the Russian Communist Party, the leader of the 1917 Bolshevik Revolution, and the architect of the Soviet state.

Lenin was born in tsarist Russia in 1870, just three years after Marx published *Das Kapital*. Lenin's parents instilled in young Vladimir a love of education and culture, as well as an unquenchable passion for reading. Cultural oppression under the tsar, however, ignited a spark of radical activism among his siblings, and the entire family eventually became involved in acts of revolution against the regime. Surrounded by radical influences, it's little wonder that Lenin became a radical early in life.

When Lenin was just seventeen, his oldest brother, Alexander, was hanged for participating in a terrorist bomb plot to assassinate Tsar Alexander III. Alexander's execution marked a critical tipping point for young Vladimir. Fueled by the bitter loss of his brother, Lenin fully embraced the Marxist creed and the revolutionary cause of communism. The painting *We Will Follow a Different Path*, which shows a grief-stricken Vladimir with his mother following Alexander's death, symbolizes this defining moment in Lenin's life.

Lenin became a disciple of Marx and Engels in the ensuing years, studying their theories and eventually translating their writings into the Russian language. Marx's book *Das Kapital* had a significant impact on Lenin's views, and in 1889, Lenin officially declared himself a Marxist-Communist. "Give us an organization of revolutionaries," Lenin later proclaimed, "and we shall overturn the whole of Russia."[12]

Like Marx and Engels, Lenin believed that if the oppressed workers of Russia became poor and hungry enough, they would rise up as one against the wealthy, plunder their riches, grab the golden egg of the tsars, and eliminate the upper classes. Then the victors would enjoy the spoils of revolution, and they would all live happily ever after.

But this lofty goal could only be accomplished by full-throttle revolution. The old, corrupt Russian system would be destroyed, along with its greed and opulence, and the glorious Communist system would take its place. In this new system, the hoarded wealth of the bourgeoisie would be redistributed to the masses through a fair and equitable plan.

After completing his law degree in 1892, Lenin moved to Saint Petersburg, Russia, and shifted his focus to revolutionary politics. He and other Marxists joined forces in calling for an overthrow of the tsar and his corrupt bourgeois system of government. Lenin's activism resulted in three years of exile in Siberia. Exile, however, only strengthened Lenin's resolve and increased his revolutionary activities.

In the early 1900s, Russia became embroiled in a bitter war with Japan, and by 1905, the economy was in shambles, the ragtag Russian army had been defeated and demoralized, and starvation had driven people into the streets, desperate for change. Conditions were ripe for a revolution. Civilians rose up in protest to petition the tsar, but the protests were brutally crushed. In an apparent attempt to appease the masses and prevent further bloodshed, the tsar quickly conceded to their demands and established a legislative assembly called the Duma, which the people would elect to represent them.

Meanwhile, Lenin sparred with other Marxists in the Social Democratic Labor Party over revolutionary ideology. Lenin argued that Russia's working class must lead the revolution against the tsarist system. The Mensheviks, however, believed that the bourgeoisie should remain in power. Eventually, Lenin and his Bolshevik comrades split off and formed their own party.

During World War I, Lenin embarked on a self-imposed exile in Switzerland, but his obsession with revolution continued unabated. In 1917, Lenin hurried back to Russia after receiving word that the tsar had been deposed and a provisional government led by the bourgeois liberals had been established. Perhaps fearing that a perfectly good revolution might go to waste, Lenin called for total revolution and a new Soviet government led by the workers, peasants, and soldiers. Again, in Lenin's view, completely overthrowing the current system was the only way to purge the corrupt influences of capitalism from the culture and usher in a Communist state. The revolution would spread throughout the world, and once the capitalist nations in the West were isolated, they would be brought to their knees, and communism would seize full control of the world.

Lenin called for peasants and workers to rise up against the bourgeoisie, and he reached out to the disenfranchised soldiers who had suffered greatly under the tsar. The revolution Lenin had dreamed of suddenly ignited into a firestorm in October of 1917. The tsar and his family were whisked away and assassinated, and all civilian opposition was crushed in a flood of brutality and genocide known as the Red Terror. The Bolshevik Revolution was a grand success, at least initially. The people rejoiced when Lenin declared Russia a Soviet Communist state. The wealth and power of the tsars now belonged to the proletariat, the peasants, and the soldiers.

Yet Lenin's dream of a nation devoid of class strife, bourgeois corruption, and capitalist greed never materialized. Under Lenin's dictatorship, famine, poverty, and misery prevailed, but Lenin merely attributed the failures of the Communist system to a government that had drifted away from the Marxist revolutionary creed.

Without the writings of Marx and Engels, Lenin might never have found a systematized basis for his brash Communist experiment. And had it not been for Lenin, the writings of Marx and Engels might have remained in the theoretical realm.

Lenin died just seven years after the October Revolution, but his Communist experiment lived on through his successor, Joseph Stalin, who proved to be even more brutal and despotic than his Marxist comrade.

It's abundantly clear that Smith and Marx, along with his protégé Lenin, were poles apart in their economic and political views. But whose theories ultimately made the world better off? The historical track records of each system offer all the evidence we need to answer that question.

Without being too simplistic, I would again point out that all of the economic and political systems in the world today fall into one of two camps: *growth* or *redistribution*. If you recall our earlier discussion, the growth camp is typically referred to as a free-market system, and the redistribution camp is known as a command system. Free-enterprise systems, which align with Adam Smith's views, have traditionally emphasized economic growth, minimal government interference, free trade, and individual freedom. Systems based on Marxism, socialism, and communism, however, advocate income redistribution and maximum government control over the economy and culture.

The redistribution camp views free enterprise as the *cause* of poverty, income inequality, and interpersonal oppression rather than the solution. The only path to prosperity and equality, it asserts, is to abolish personal wealth and property (which presumably eliminates greed), redistribute wealth equally among the members of a society, and place all economic, political, and social control in the hands of the state. The political experiments of the past two hundred years are largely an outgrowth of the tensions between these two camps.

Is the growth or free-market system the cause of poverty and oppression as

Socialists and Communists claim? Is the command or redistribution system the sole cure for poverty and inequality?

Let's examine both systems under the microscope and see how they measure up in a toe-to-toe comparison. I think we'll find that only one system has consistently passed the test when it comes to making people better off.

THE REDISTRIBUTION CAMP

The proponents of Marxism, socialism, and communism are unified in condemning capitalism and the free-enterprise system for causing poverty, class warfare, and oppression. They believe that the greed-infested capitalist system is rotten to the core and must be abolished. In their zeal to save the world, they outlaw the free market and impose a redistributive system of government.

In theory, the Marxist-Communist camp has lofty goals to promote peace, equality, and prosperity through redistribution. But how does redistribution measure up in the real world?

Let's review the essentials of the Marxist-Communist system:

1. All property is collectively owned, and entrepreneurship is abolished. Private property and wealth are redistributed "from each according to his ability to each according to his need," as determined by the state.

2. A centralized, authoritarian government operates by arbitrary rule. The state controls all economic activity, including production, labor, prices, and wages. The free-market components of profit and loss, competition, and economic freedom of choice are abolished.

3. The state strictly limits or forbids cultural freedom of choice. All aspects of an individual's life, including education, career, housing, and food allotment, are under the control and direction of the state. The state also strictly limits or forbids religious freedom.

In a redistribution system, the all-wise, all-powerful government owns and controls everything. No one is burdened with encumbrances like individual wealth, private property, or family inheritance. No one has to worry about economic volatility or greedy and exploitative businesses because the state controls every bank, factory, business, utility, housing program, and school. A nation's wealth and property are "equitably" allocated as the state sees fit.

Yet for all its emphasis on equity, the redistribution system is anything but fair. Under such a system no one ends up better off, except perhaps for the intellectual elites running the country. The only thing that's assured is equal poverty and misery for all.

What's Mine Is Yours

On the surface, collective ownership of property and the redistribution of wealth sound much more fair and equitable than allowing greedy, selfish individuals to hoard their wealth and property while the less fortunate suffer. The redistribution camp believes that people must be compelled to do the right thing and spread their wealth around. Left to themselves, individuals will never voluntarily overcome their selfish tendencies. But the state is perfectly empowered to assist in this altruistic endeavor. The system is designed so that those who have more than they need will relinquish their excess wealth to those who have less than they need. Then everything will be equal, all things considered.

But the truth is, when government promises to take away from those who have earned wealth and redistribute that wealth to those who didn't earn it, they are appealing to the selfishness of the recipients, who gain from the efforts of others rather than from their own efforts.

Private ownership is also anathema to the Marxist-Communists, who believe that it instigates class warfare and promotes greed. The simple solution, of course, is to abolish private ownership in favor of collectivism. If everyone owns everything—under the benevolent control of the state, of course—equality will be assured. Greed and class warfare will instantly vanish.

But what is considered equitable and fair in a redistribution system is actually theft. As humans, we innately sense that stealing is wrong. We were taught that "You shall not steal." Theft committed by a government entity is just as much stealing as theft between individuals, though it may be easier to hide or justify.

Marx and his camp erroneously assumed the state could eliminate greed, poverty, and class warfare by government decree. But as history bears out, these societal ills are still alive and well in Socialist and Communist systems. Arbitrarily spreading the wealth around leaves everyone worse off and does nothing to rid the human heart of greed, selfishness, or covetousness.

Let's consider the concept of equality for a moment. The redistributionist's idea of equality has to do with outcomes, not opportunity. It's one thing to give everyone an equal chance to succeed (or fail), but Socialists and Communists insist that the playing field must be level, and everyone must receive the same reward. Ensuring equal outcomes is the only way everyone can become better off. In reality, however, it's an appallingly unfair approach that ultimately destroys ingenuity, innovation, and a healthy work ethic.

As I noted earlier, a functioning economy must produce goods and services to generate income. Wealth is built on production, which stimulates growth. Redistribution, however, is built on a model of economic *contraction*. Marx and Lenin failed to factor growth into the economic equation, so the redistribution system provides no incentive to develop *new sources* of wealth. Like a leech, redistribution sucks away at a nation's wealth until the economy shrivels up and goes bankrupt. Redistribution has never worked over the long haul. Wealth can only be redistributed so many times before the money runs out.

The Pitfalls of Central Planning

Karl Marx and his comrades had great faith in the state but no faith in individuals to govern themselves. As Marx stated so revealingly, the class struggle necessarily leads to the "dictatorship of the proletariat."[1] Government alone was wise enough to run everything and knew best how to manage the economic, political, and cultural spheres of society. Under the state's benevolent oversight, there would be peace, equality, security, and abundance for everyone.

Marx and Lenin presumed that centralized, authoritarian governments would be capable of micromanaging their economies to the minutest detail. They scoffed disdainfully at capital investments, profits and losses, and free-market indicators. In their view, it would be a simple matter to regulate such things as supply and demand, production, prices, and wages in the marketplace.

In retrospect, Lenin's economic strategy for the 1917 revolution was pathetic and, indeed, almost laughable. The Communist coterie knew nothing about economics, much less running a business, a nation, or the world. They were so obsessed with overthrowing the tsar's regime and capturing his golden egg, they never gave any serious thought to how they would manage the economy if their plot succeeded. *What does a dog do when he finally catches the car he's been chasing?*

The junta was convinced that once they captured the regime's treasure, they'd just take control of the banks and redistribute the booty. Business would simply run the way it always did, only they would own it, not the bourgeoisie. Marx and his comrades were convinced that business owners cheated their workers and stole the profits that rightly belonged to them. In Marx's simplistic view, the value of a product should be determined only by the *value of the labor*. So the worker alone was entitled to the proceeds. But Marx and Lenin misunderstood how the real world works. Neither realized that the value of a product must factor in expenses such as rent, utilities, and the purchase of raw materials. Since they would own everything, they figured they could simply ignore these factors.

Eventually it dawned on Lenin and the revolutionaries that some economic management would be required following their bloody revolution. So the all-wise politburo came up with an economic strategy called the *Gosplan*, which means "government plan" in Russian. The Gosplan established economic strategy, the *Gosten* figured out and set prices, the *Gosnab* determined the allocation of supplies, and the *Gostude* handled wages and labor assignments. It seemed to be a right tidy management package.

The Gosplan was designed as a five-year production model, but the plan never worked. So it was reduced to a one-year plan, but that didn't work either. The truth is that the Communists and Socialists have never figured it out. To this day, Russia still bears the scars of inefficiency, supply shortages, and lost opportunity, and yet the government stubbornly rejects the principles of efficient production that lead to abundance. What arrogance to think that one tiny, centralized group of intellectuals could successfully manage trillions of complex details across an entire economy. It's an administrative nightmare.

Armenia is a prime example. On one visit I stood in a very large building that had once been a Soviet-operated leather-processing and shoe-manufacturing plant. The Soviets had long since returned to Russia, but some of the old Armenian workers had reopened the factory as a free-market enterprise. When I asked them how the Gosplan had worked under the Communists, they laughed and said, "It didn't!"

In its infinite wisdom, the Gosplan had assigned workers to different aspects of production. Some workers stamped a pattern on the shoe leather, some cut out the leather pieces, some sewed the tops of the shoes together, and some stitched the soles onto the uppers and nailed on the heels. Others dyed the shoes, dried them, and packed them in large crates to be shipped off and stored in warehouses. Everyone had a quota to meet.

But more often than not, supply shortages or equipment failures brought production to a standstill. The Armenian workers just sat around and sipped vodka. It wasn't their problem if someone down the line or up the line messed up.

Gosplan miscalculations were typically at the root of the problems. The farmers didn't have enough hay to feed their animals. The processing plants didn't have enough animals to kill and skin. The workers didn't receive enough leather to make the shoes.

Whenever something went wrong with the Gosplan, everyone down the line of production had to wait for someone to revise the plan. The workers, however, were not concerned about meeting their required quotas. They received the same housing, the same clothing, the same allotment of bread, and the same measured handful of vegetables whether they produced any shoes or not. Their comrade overseers promised that if they worked harder, things would get better. But the Armenian workers weren't fooled. They had no incentive to work harder. Why should they sacrifice when the state was already giving them everything they needed? They would merely say to each other, "As long as the comrades pretend they are paying us a decent wage, we will pretend that we are working a decent shift."

Life in Utopia

Imagine for a moment what actually happened in the aftermath of Lenin's 1917 Bolshevik Revolution. Put yourself in the shoes of the Russian people. Just think how they must have felt when life as they knew it was transformed forever. As Lenin and his new regime systematically dismantled and destroyed every economic and political system, Russian culture was torn to shreds. The oppressed masses had cheered when Lenin declared that all wealth and personal property were under new ownership. The tsar's golden egg now belonged to them.

But when Lenin embarked on his grand experiment, the people lost the most valuable commodity of all: freedom of choice. The all-powerful state would now determine what and how much people would buy, where they would live, what they would eat and wear, what they would read, what their education and careers would be, and even what they would think or talk about. Religious, cultural, economic, and individual freedoms vanished overnight. All that mattered now was the collective, not the individual. The Russian people could never have anticipated that Lenin's lofty vision would transform into a nightmare.

On the economic side of the cultural-economic matrix, the components of land, labor, capital, and the entrepreneur were no longer ruled by market factors and individual decisions. The government took over ownership and control of the *land*. *Labor* and work were directed ultimately by the politburo—that handful of elite intellectuals who exercised total control over the masses. All *capital*, including personal property, livestock, machinery, equipment, and furniture, was now owned and managed by the politburo as well. Citizens had no say in how their former wealth was redistributed. As for the *entrepreneur* … there was no such thing. The state would micromanage the economy from now on.

On the cultural side of the matrix, *traditions* were abolished, and the *institutions* that passed on those traditions no longer legally existed. The *family* was restructured, and the *individual* was melded into the seamless whole of the Communist Party. Equality of outcomes was now the name of the game. Freedom of individual choice vanished overnight.

When I think about the profound transformation that took place when Lenin imposed the Soviet system on the Russian people, I'm reminded of a scene in the film *Doctor Zhivago*.[2]

Dr. Zhivago had been away from home, conscripted to serve in the Red Army and treat the wounded soldiers on the battlefield. When he finally returned to Moscow, a surprise was awaiting him at home. A houseful of newly entitled citizens had taken "equal possession" of his property, since personal possessions no longer existed in the new order. Dr. Zhivago, his wife, and her parents were permitted to use a very small portion of the home as their living quarters. When the new inhabitants discovered that the good doctor was going to burn some of his own wood in his own small stove, they were outraged and discussed whether they should hold a tribunal. The house no longer belonged to Dr. Zhivago, nor did the wood or the stove.

The movie paints a graphic picture of life in the new Soviet state. Everything was redistributed, but no one was better off. Instead, it brought out the very worst in people. Yet by the time they realized what Lenin's glorious Communist system was doing to their country, it was too late.

The Infection Spreads

The same diseased redistribution system infected Asia as well. Yet in recent years, the Chinese have been trying to rediscover the secrets to efficiency and abundance in the aftermath of the Cultural Revolution and their bout with communism. Unfortunately, North Korea is still suffering under the delusion that the redistributive Communist system will one day lead to peace and prosperity.

I recall riding in an automobile near Sinuiju City on one of my trips to North Korea. As I gazed at the countryside quilted with rice paddies and rectangular concrete houses, I was plagued by a menacing thought. Finally, I risked asking one of the Communist leaders a probing question.

"This is beautiful land for agriculture," I began. "I suppose that before the Marxist revolution, four or five generations of Korean families owned it in succession. When Great Leader Kim Il-Sung announced that they no longer owned the land and then tore down their homes, insisting that everyone move into rectangular concrete buildings, how did these families respond?"

"Oh, it was a wonderful day" was the official's scripted reply. "Dr. Jackson, there is no way you can understand how eager everyone was to respond to Great Leader's glorious announcement that now no one owned anything, but everyone owned everything. From that day on, Great Leader Kim Il-Sung would personally take care of all of our needs. No one would be in want of anything. They were all so happy to move into their new homes with others who would be tending the communal rice fields with them."

After that conversation, I quietly continued my research and discovered that the state "graciously" allowed family members a single hint of protest over surrendering their inheritance. Then they were murdered. Oddly enough, rice production at that point fed a higher percentage of the population than before. Since then, the population has not only decreased, but rice production has dwindled to the point where there isn't enough rice to feed the North Korean people, much less sell to eager international buyers.

Redistribution, in theory, sounds like an equitable plan that would make everyone better off. If the wealth is spread around, no one will be poor or live in want of basic necessities. But if we scratch beneath the veneer of Communist systems, as in the case of North Korea, we find that despite all their coercive efforts to enforce redistributive mandates, no one actually ends up better off. The redistribution camp has no solutions for the problem of poverty or the elusive quest for prosperity.

The social progressives in power in the United States today are no less mistaken than the Communist leaders of Russia, China, and North Korea. The hallmarks of a redistribution mentality can be seen just as clearly in the Western world: the increasingly repressive government infringements on individual choice, the contemptible violation of property rights, the systematic dismantling of the free-enterprise system, the outrageous interference with healthy competition, and the flagrant abuse of reasonable taxation.

The results are the same whether an outrageous redistribution plot begins with a Lenin-type revolution or a more insidious and intellectualized 1930s-style "new deal." Only the timing is different. Political leaders in either scenario make grandiose promises and offer a host of enticements, benefits, and handouts to constituents in exchange for their vote in a democratic election or their support in a revolution. Free government goodies ensure that the politburo—the political elites of a nation—will inherit power and control over the nation's purse strings.

A Model of Peace, Equality, and Prosperity?

As history has demonstrated time and again, when Marxist theory becomes reality, it inevitably leaves a trail of destruction, poverty, and suffering in its wake. As I mentioned earlier, some notable consequences of the Communists' impassioned efforts to eliminate free-enterprise economies and impose redistributive systems can still be seen in places like the old Soviet Union and North Korea. But I also witnessed the tragic results of redistribution in many other countries I've visited: millions of people starved, valuable resources were wasted, economies were devastated, sectarian violence was quelled by brute force, and people's lives were reduced to a meager existence.

When incentives to voluntarily participate in the Communists' grand social experiment faded away, punishment, torture, and genocide enforced the desired political or economic goals. No one—except perhaps the elite politburo members arbitrarily making the rules—was better off in the end. The redistribution system clearly isn't the model of peace, equality, and prosperity that it claims to be.

Let's see if the growth camp performs any better under scrutiny.

THE GROWTH CAMP

Throughout history, people have made choices in their own interests to survive and prosper, but critics have regarded individual freedom of choice with scorn and suspicion. As I noted earlier, the redistribution camp claims that free enterprise and capitalism are the cause of poverty, inequality, and oppression. Not surprisingly, they're quick to point out the inequities and weaknesses of the economic-growth system. To hear them talk, you'd think that greed, corruption, and self-interest originated with capitalism. But the redistribution camp is silent when it comes to the successful track record of the growth system in uprooting poverty and cultivating prosperity.

Are the criticisms of free enterprise justified? Are greed and self-interest truly at the heart of capitalism? To answer these questions, we need to first understand what the free-enterprise system is and how it works.

The Key to Prosperity

Advocates of the growth system view *individual liberty* as an essential component of wealth creation and the key to prosperity. Adam Smith observed that if a nation allows individuals to exercise economic and cultural freedom of choice within a legal framework of fairness and the rule of law, those individuals will spontaneously use their God-given abilities to produce goods and services.[1] Wealth will flow from their productivity, and the economy will grow to make everyone better off. That's the basic idea behind the free-enterprise system.

When industrious people have the freedom to prosper individually, a nation will thrive. But a corrupt, authoritarian government that steals the fruits of conscientious labor from its citizens through excessive taxation or coercive redistribution will reap civil unrest, unemployment, increased crime, and poverty.

In his travels as a tutor, Smith identified some essential principles that wealthy nations embraced:[2]

1. The right for individuals to own private property and control the means of production, including labor.

2. The freedom of individuals to enter voluntarily into contractual agreements and engage in trade and business with minimal government interference. This included allowing market forces to determine prices and wages.

3. The right to limited government that operated under the rule of law. This included the individual right to equal opportunity and fair treatment under the law.

4. The freedom of individuals to make economic choices in the marketplace that might result in profit (or loss).

5. The freedom of individuals to make personal choices within a cultural system that promoted and protected individual rights and liberty.

As Smith observed, nations that promoted freedom clearly prospered, while impoverished nations lacked this essential element. Let's take a closer look at the key principles of free enterprise.

The Beauty of Freedom

Close your eyes for a moment and imagine a world of abundant opportunity and liberty in which you're free to pursue your dreams and use your gifts and abilities to the fullest. Imagine being the sole proprietor of your wealth and possessions, harnessing and allocating all the resources at your disposal as you see fit.

Now imagine a government that exists solely to protect and promote your rights and the freedom to choose a personal path to becoming better off. Imagine a world in which your initiative, hard work, and ingenuity are rewarded—a world in which you are a creator, not just a consumer. As the fruits of your labor increase, you can grow and expand, including others in your endeavor, so they can become better off as well.

Freedom is at the heart of the great American experiment. The men who founded this nation fought to secure individual liberty to pursue one's own interests and become better off. The freedom to choose is a precious gift we should never take for granted.

I think it's fair to say that the American experiment succeeded beyond the founders' wildest dreams. Walk into any department store around the nation, and you'll discover an overwhelming array of products. Compared with the scarcity of goods in redistributive economies like the former Soviet Union, America is truly blessed. Where did all these products come from? The answer is clear: individuals pursuing their own interests, harnessing their own resources, producing what others want or need, generating wealth, and making themselves and others better off. No other system in the world has replicated this formula for success and prosperity the way America has. History has proven that growth is the path to becoming better off, and the key to that growth is freedom.

The beauty of free enterprise is that every individual has the exclusive right to own private property, which may include real estate or land, as well as personal possessions, accumulated wealth, and family inheritance. Property ownership is the fundamental basis for free enterprise, and property owners have the right to transfer or dispose of their property as they see fit.

In a free-enterprise system, one of your most valuable possessions is your ability to work. You are entitled to exchange your labor for income or other benefits.

You have the freedom to enter into contracts or agreements voluntarily, but you must also accept the associated risks. In any business endeavor, there is a possibility of succeeding or failing. When free enterprise functions the way it was originally designed, there are always winners and losers, and no business is too big to fail. Government doesn't pick winners and losers or dictate who can enter into a contract.

Individual freedom extends to making choices that will enrich and improve our lives and increase our wealth. But a free-enterprise system works only if everyone abides by the rule of law. The law must apply to everyone equally, including those in authority. Laws must be authoritative, just, and enforceable, but they must also be predictable. Arbitrary lawmaking violates the rule of law, which requires everyone to play by the same rules. When two individuals enter into a voluntary agreement, they assume that some kind of authoritative establishment will enforce that agreement fairly and predictably.

The Invisible Hand

As we discussed earlier, Marx and Lenin failed to understand or accept that freedom is the lifeblood of a healthy economic system. They believed that the free market promoted inequality, exploitation, and poverty, and that state control was necessary to ensure fairness and promote prosperity. So they sought to abolish free enterprise.

Adam Smith, however, reached the opposite conclusion in his research. To him, the free market was an intriguing system of diverse and intricate complexities that combined to produce a functioning and buoyant economy. Market forces were invisible and spontaneous, and the delicate interplay between them could not be controlled or coerced. In a very real sense, these forces were wild and free.

Smith observed, for example, that *prices are the nervous system of a free-enterprise system*. When prices are established through individual transactions in a free market, silent signals are transmitted to the entire economic system. Those signals—the "invisible hand,"[3] as Smith called them—inform and guide the actions of millions of other individuals in the system without anyone else telling them what to do.

Milton Friedman incisively explained the three functions of prices in his book *Free to Choose*:

> First, [prices] transmit information; second, they provide an incentive to adopt those methods of production that are least costly and thereby use available resources for the most highly valued purposes; third, they determine who gets how much of the product—the distribution of income.[4]

At some point in a business transaction, the seller and the buyer reach a juncture where they're ready to strike a deal. If they reach an agreement, the price for a product or service is established. A successful transaction makes both of them feel they're coming out of the deal better off. It also encourages them to enter into more transactions to feel better off again and again. Repeated transactions expand the total economy.

In a free-enterprise system, prices balance the demand for goods and services with supply so there aren't huge shortages or surpluses. The quantity consumers want to purchase is assured to match the quantity producers want to sell. The balance between supply and demand is no accident. Prices make it come out right each time—unless some controlling government entity interferes. Even in stormy economic conditions, goods and services in a free-enterprise system are available at the current market price.

Let's say that a retailer strikes a deal with a shoe manufacturer for a specified number of shoes at a certain price. The manufacturer delays ordering the leather he needs for the job, and in the interim, a drought creates a supply shortage. Immediately a signal circulates throughout the marketplace, and the price of leather in the system goes up. A cattleman in Texas hears about the leather shortage and decides to sell most of his cattle to the shoe industry rather than the steak market in Japan. His neighbor also hears the news and decides to raise cattle next year, instead of growing sorghum, in hopes of making a handsome profit.

The leather shortage also means that the price of shoes will go up, and customers will have to decide whether or not to pay the higher price. Since the shoe retailer had a firm contract with the shoe manufacturer to purchase the product at a lower price, he can either make a bigger profit from raising his shoe prices or sell his shoes faster at a lower price.

But the procrastinating shoe manufacturer has a problem. If he can't find some leather at last year's price, he'll sustain a loss. So he scans the commodities page in the *Wall Street Journal* and finds a leather supplier in Brazil who is willing to sell him the leather at last year's price. With his losses covered, the shoe manufacturer can fulfill his contract with the retailer.

These market signals and decisions happened almost instantaneously, without the need for a government entity to gather, sort, analyze, and disseminate the information. Everyone who had an economic stake in the leather and shoe industries had free access to all the information they needed to make decisions in their best interests.

That's the beauty of free enterprise.

Win a Little, Lose a Little

Profits have gotten a bad rap in a world where corporate greed makes the headlines on a daily basis. Yet without the possibility of making a profit, few people would run the risk of establishing a business. And without businesses, the goods and services we need and enjoy wouldn't be available.

Profit isn't inherently evil; it's simply an indicator of economic growth. Profits inform us of the positive value added to the economy, which is sometimes referred to as the gross domestic product (GDP).

Let's say a tech company in California's Silicon Valley manufactures computer chips from granules of sand. The expense of transforming sand into a marketable product is the company's *cost of production*. The computer chips are then sold in the marketplace at an agreed-upon price. The difference between the production costs and the sales price is the company's *profit*. That newly generated profit not only increases the nation's wealth but can also grow more wealth. That's how the growth system works.

Signals that promote growth are inherent in the free-enterprise system. Like the invisible hand that regulates prices, these signals happen spontaneously. Simple market forces guide individuals to use natural resources in the most efficient way possible. Collective consumer purchases direct resources to businesses that are meeting expectations and away from businesses that aren't. If strong product sales generate a profit, businesses receive an automatic signal that they should continue selling a product.

In a free-enterprise economy, even high profits send important signals that attract other players to the industry. As new businesses enter the marketplace, *competition* increases, which naturally forces prices and profits down and promotes efficiency in the system. Isn't it interesting that profits encourage the very competition that keeps them in check?

Like profits, *losses* also send important signals in a free-enterprise system. Businesses must match their production choices with consumer desires or face losses and eventual bankruptcy. Losses are painful, but in the long haul, they can yield rewards if they bring about change and a more efficient use of resources.

Just as high profits signal new businesses to get involved in an industry, losses signal businesses to make changes or close their doors. When expenses exceed profits, a business is in trouble and must change its approach or risk failure. Failure simply means that a business isn't making people better off. When one business fails, other businesses have the opportunity to manage the resources more effectively to make people better off. If those businesses succeed, the profits they generate will encourage competition, which will regulate prices and profits.

That ubiquitous invisible hand in the free-enterprise system is always working behind the scenes guiding individuals who are merely exercising their freedom of choice while acting in their own best interests.

An Honest Wage

Adam Smith wisely perceived that "a man must always live by his work, and his wages must at least be sufficient to maintain him."[5] Wages typically refer to the compensation individuals receive from their labor. At one time, laborers received all the fruits of their labor from working their own land. But eventually they had to rent their land and subtract the expense from their gross compensation. The cost of capital improvements, such as tools, equipment, and livestock, had to be subtracted from their compensation as well.

Today the government reaches into workers' pockets and deducts income taxes, Social Security, and Medicare from gross wages. The amount left over is their take-home pay, which is further reduced by other taxes and fees. Employers must pay a portion of their employees' tax bills—Social Security and Medicare—on top of their own taxes, and self-employed individuals must shoulder the entire tax burden. A nibble here and a nibble there, and wages quickly become a scarce commodity.

In a free-enterprise economy, there is a natural tension between the employee and the employer when it comes to wages. Adam Smith noted,

> The common wages of labour … [depend] everywhere upon the contract usually made between those two parties, whose interests are by no means the same. The workmen desire to get as much, the masters to give as little, as possible. The former are disposed to combine in order to raise, the latter in order to lower, the wages of labour.[6]

Ultimately, productivity determines wages. The value of what is produced is reflected in the wage paid to produce it. Those invisible market forces Smith described immediately send out signals that influence business decisions. If a firm pays a wage that exceeds the value a worker produces, it will quickly go out of business. What signal tells a company that it's paying less than the value a worker produces? The beautiful and efficient concept called *competition*.

If a business is paying a worker ten dollars per hour, but the value the worker is producing exceeds twenty-five dollars per hour, a competitor in the same industry will offer that worker nearly twice as much as she is presently earning and snatch her away from her present employer. Fair wages in a competitive market reflect the productivity of the labor so that everyone in a free-market system ends up better off.

Systems Really Do Matter

In all the countries I've visited over the years in my work with Project C.U.R.E., I've listened with deep sadness to the heart cries of people who would give almost anything to enjoy the advantages Americans take for granted. Yet when I return to the United States, I find it even more heartbreaking that my fellow citizens understand so little about our nation and don't seem to realize or care that we're losing our economic and cultural advantages. They don't seem to understand that more of our wealth and freedom are being whittled away each time our government imposes another layer of taxes, fees, and bureaucratic regulations. These onerous taxes and regulations stifle production and dry up all the resources necessary for wealth creation.

We must never forget that our nation has enjoyed success and prosperity largely because its founders believed in freedom. Freedom of economic and cultural choice promotes the initiative, creativity, and productivity necessary for wealth creation and growth. In a free system, everybody ends up better off.

The United States and Great Britain started out with economic systems built on freedom of choice. As a result, production flourished, industrial revolutions took place, and wealth was generated. But then governments began tinkering with the formula for prosperity. In all their tinkering, they failed to consider the positive correlation between wealth and freedom of economic and cultural choice. Somewhere along the line, they forgot that the secret of prosperity resides in an economic system that promotes freedom and enables individuals to not only create wealth without coercion but keep the fruits of their labor.

Adam Smith concluded that the

> security which the laws in Great Britain give to every man, that he shall enjoy the fruits of his own labour, is alone sufficient to make any country flourish. … The natural effort of every individual to better his own condition, when [allowed] to exert itself with freedom and security, is so powerful a principle, that it is alone, and without any assistance … capable of carrying on the society to wealth and prosperity.[7]

Once again we see that freedom is the key to prosperity. The great American experiment of 1776 secured these blessings for us, but sadly our wealth has been squandered in profligate spending, astronomic debt, burdensome regulation, and outrageous politics. Our system of growth has transformed before our very eyes into a system of redistribution. We have strayed from the path so sacrificially laid out for us and have embraced the slippery theory of bathtub economics.

Systems really do matter, and so do our choices. We can continue down a redistributive path that will inevitably lead to poverty, or we can retrace our steps toward growth and prosperity. Here comes that same old question: What'cha gonna do with what'cha got?

18

★ ★ ★

ANSWERING THE CRITICS

So, what about the scathing criticisms of capitalism and the free-enterprise system? I would say that much of the outrage I hear about the greed, exploitation, and self-interest inherent in the growth system is based on misinformation, misunderstanding, or manipulation of the facts. And there's no better way to deal with misinformation than to confront it with the truth. In this chapter, I'll briefly respond to the two most frequent criticisms coming from the redistribution camp today.

"Free Enterprise Is Just Another Form of Selfishness."

In his book *The Wealth of Nations*, Adam Smith observed that the economic systems of wealthy countries promoted freedom of choice that enabled individuals to pursue their own interests. But Smith made another intriguing discovery: as individuals pursued and enhanced their own interests, the interests of others were simultaneously enhanced.

Smith concluded that the individual pursuit of self-interest unintentionally benefits society as a whole. In other words, "it is not from the benevolence of the butcher, the brewer, or the baker that we expect our dinner, but from their regard to their own interest."[1]

No exchange will take place between two parties unless cooperation is voluntary, and both parties benefit from the deal. Everyone has to end up better off. That's why, as Smith noted, those entering into a deal may intend only their own individual gain, but like an "invisible hand," they unintentionally end up promoting the other person's gain as well.

I discovered years ago in my own Jackson Brothers Investments dealings that to ensure a successful business deal, it was more beneficial to emphasize the advantages the client would experience by agreeing to our deal, rather than talking about my needs or advantages. A deal must be good for *both parties*, or it won't be successful.

In redistribution systems, individuals are told that if they work hard and sacrifice for the collective, they will eventually end up better off. But their cooperation must often be ensured through coercion. We would be hard pressed to find a secular institution that has ever successfully induced individuals to voluntarily sacrifice their self-interests for the glory of the collective.

In hippie communes, for example, individuals will work for the collective good as long as they get what they signed up for. They will calculate precisely what they feel their physical and mental capital is worth in the deal. The promise of some distant reward won't convince them to make a bad deal. Everyone in the deal must end up better off, or the deal will fall apart. The hippies in the commune may waste a few years of their lives chasing the illusion of greater glory, but eventually they'll walk away from the painted hippie bus.

When Adam Smith introduced the concept of self-interest in his writings, he laid himself wide open to misunderstanding, misinterpretation, and criticism. Those in the redistribution camp might easily dismiss him as a greedy scoundrel, a champion of selfishness, or a bourgeois capitalist interested only in exploiting and stealing from the poor. But those accusations are completely unjustified. Let's look at what Smith actually wrote:

> The obvious and simple system of natural liberty establishes itself of its own accord. Every man, as long as he does not violate the laws of justice, is left perfectly free to pursue his own interest his own way, and to bring both his industry and capital into competition with those of any other man, or order

of men. The sovereign is completely discharged from … the duty of super-intending the industry of private people, and of directing it towards the employments most suitable to the interest of the society.[2]

Smith presumed that every person wants to end up better off in life. If an individual was allowed, according to the "system of natural liberty," to pursue voluntary transactions with other free individuals, the transactions would be successful only if both trading partners ended up better off. This system would encourage additional transactions and greatly increase the volume of successful business.

Granted, the human desire to end up better off can lead to selfishness. However, the desire to make good decisions and end up better off in life demonstrates good stewardship and reveals our willingness to accept personal responsibility. *Selfishness* is an attitude in which an individual places arbitrary demands on others regardless of the cost to them. A selfish, demanding attitude that insists "It's all about me!" is counterproductive because all the parties involved don't end up better off. That's why Smith emphasized that government, and those who serve in government, must not be greedy or selfish either. Greed is always counterproductive to everyone becoming better off.

To control the government's tendency toward greed, Smith built checks and balances into the free-enterprise system, limiting the sovereign (king) to (1) "protecting the society from the violence and invasion of other independent societies," (2) "protecting … every member of the society from the injustice or oppression of every other member," and (3) "erecting and maintaining certain public works and … institutions" that would be too costly for individuals to maintain (e.g., courts, public records, road systems, etc.).[3]

Government can easily induce its constituents to believe the promise that it can make them better off through grants, subsidies, and other favors. But those promises of government largesse are a myth. It's delusional to think that government alone generates and controls the nation's wealth and has the right to distribute it to whomever submits to its dictates. Government doesn't earn any of the money it promises to give away; rather, to give away money, it has to take it from individuals who have already earned it. Promises of favors, grants, and subsidies are a way of buying off constituents. Politicians think that by appealing to the selfishness of the recipients, they will garner votes so they can remain in power. Sadly, this tactic is very effective.

Thomas Jefferson and Adam Smith both envisioned government in the role of an umpire, not a participant, in the marketplace. They believed that individuals in a free nation should be able to pursue their own interests and values, and that those pursuits, which could be neither greedy nor selfish, were necessary for everyone to end up better off.

"Capitalism Is Infested with Greed and Corruption"

Two subjects that triggered the ravings of Karl Marx and Friedrich Engels were *profit* and *capital*. As we discussed earlier, the redistribution camp abolished profit. They reasoned that if workers (the proletariat) owned, produced, and distributed everything, there would be no need for profit, and all the workers would have more.

The redistributionists also totally misunderstood the concepts of capital and capitalism. They thought it had to do with class warfare and the conflict between workers and owners. They believed that the bourgeois capitalist owners were exploiting and stealing from their workers. Consequently, the redistribution camp wanted to do away with every capitalist and anything that smacked of capitalism.

Capitalists can indeed be greedy, corrupt, and in league with the government to gain a business advantage, but capitalism itself isn't the cause of greed or exploitation. *Capital* simply refers to "stuff." It has to do with more than just money. It can refer to equipment and tools of the trade, land, real estate, labor, goods, and other assets. Economists refer to *human capital*, for example, as the set of skills and experiences a worker brings to the marketplace. An individual can increase his or her human capital through continuing education, advanced training, or years of experience in a certain field.

Any kind of capital, including human capital, increases a worker's ability to produce at a higher level and thus increases the likelihood of a higher wage. For instance, when a construction worker increases his productivity by investing in appropriate tools for his job, he increases his wage-earning value in the marketplace. Marx simply didn't get the concept that the stock of capital at a worker's disposal increases productivity and the possibility of increased wages. All that inflammatory rhetoric about capitalism was no doubt a useful political ploy to fan the flames of revolution.

When governments impede the activity and growth of business through a system of redistribution, oppressive regulations and restrictions, or higher taxes, the result is fewer profits. This translates to less money for capital infusion, less productivity, fewer wage increases, fewer distribution possibilities, and less wealth generation, which prevents individuals and the nation as a whole from becoming better off.

But when business owners are free to invest capital in their ventures, they can greatly boost the efficiency and profitability of their enterprises. This infusion of capital increases productivity, and higher productivity leads to higher wages. Higher productivity can also result in higher distribution possibilities that can increase profits and allow for additional infusions of capital. As businesses grow, they hire more workers, and everybody ends up better off.

Contrary to the redistribution system, where everything shrinks and no one ends up better off, what is good for the capitalist is also good for the worker.

19

★ ★ ★

THE EROSION OF
FREE ENTERPRISE

When I speak about free enterprise and the importance of cultural and economic freedom of choice, people sometimes think I believe that the United States still holds to the principles set forth in 1776. The truth is, we did … but we don't anymore.

As we discussed earlier, our growth-based system started getting jumbled around 1929 when the nation spiraled into the Great Depression. The cozy collaboration between Franklin D. Roosevelt and English economist John Maynard Keynes led our country by leaps and bounds down the path toward Marxist socialism and a centralized economic system.

The same voluptuous temptation that snared Marx, Engels, and Lenin enticed Americans into believing that they could live at the expense of others. That great mirage of promised wealth redistribution was powerful enough to buy FDR the political support and votes he coveted.

The nation's transformation from a constitutional republic based on free enterprise to a redistributive Socialist system didn't happen through some violent, Bolshevik-style revolution. But the subtle bending of the American spine has achieved the same goals over time. In the beginning, the changes appeared innocent, but in retrospect, it's easy to see the machinations of corrupt political institutions manipulating people and events behind the scenes.

Following the Great Depression, Keynes continued pressuring Roosevelt to centralize America's economic system so the government would control everything, doling out economic favors and subsidies to citizens, whose increased dependence on the state would guarantee future votes.

There are hundreds of instances in which the US government has manipulated economic philosophy and policies to gain and maintain centralized control of the economy. Not to pick on farmers, but one excellent example of this subtle form of political manipulation is US farm policy. American farming is such a basic, straightforward way to make a living, it's hard to believe that our agricultural industry has been undermined. But decades of government tinkering with farm policy have been enormously destructive, and the American family farm as we once knew it has all but vanished from the landscape. Let's take a closer look at how this happened.

The Great American Farm

In the 1930s, farming families comprised about 25 percent of the US population.[1] A voting bloc that large was just too juicy to ignore, so FDR declared that farming was a fundamental American institution that should be nurtured as a way of life. Moreover, since farms were subject to extraordinary hazards—like floods, insects, and droughts—they simply couldn't exist without government help.

So the government guaranteed taxpayer subsidies for farmers, as well as consistently higher prices for their products to protect them from loss and low income. "And by the way," said the politicians, "we'd appreciate your continued support so these amenities won't be taken away from you."

Politicians have a shrewd understanding of human nature, and they know that once someone begins to receive a subsidy, it's almost impossible to break the addiction. Eventually, recipients develop an attitude of entitlement.

An outrageous letter from a Texas farmer to his congressman is a fitting example. In the letter, the farmer boldly stated,

My friend … received a $1,000 check from the government this year for not raising [50] hogs. So, I am going into the not-raising-hogs business next year. … I plan to operate on a small scale at first, holding myself down to [not raising] about 4,000 hogs, which means I will have $80,000 coming from the government.[2]

What farmer with half a brain would look a gift horse in the mouth?

If buying votes hadn't been the real issue, government "assistance" would never have been necessary. The invisible hand of the free-enterprise system would have informed farmers what crops to plant, how much to plant, where to buy the seed, and where to sell at the exact and right price.

Tinkering with Supply

Since the 1930s, our government has supported agriculture with a plethora of farm programs and subsidies, including:

- income and price subsidies,
- agriculture research,
- farm credit,
- water and soil programs,
- crop insurance, and
- giant subsidies for farm exports.

Roosevelt's Agricultural Adjustment Act of 1933 was based on the *parity concept*: if a farmer sold a bushel of corn in 1912 for enough money to buy a shirt, he should be able to sell a bushel of corn at any *future* date for enough money to buy a shirt. The stability and security of that policy really appealed to farm families. If the price of shirts tripled over time, then the price of their corn would also triple—guaranteed. They would vote for FDR forever.

That empty-headed logic may have bought Roosevelt votes, but it didn't buy him a Nobel Prize in economics. Over the years, economists have uniformly rejected the parity notion. There's no logic in the proposition that a farmer should be able to buy a shirt for a bushel of corn at any time. The relative value of goods and services is established by supply and demand. When technology changes or new resources or products appear on the scene or styles or tastes change, relative values also change.

But to ensure parity, the US government was forced to impose *price supports* and arbitrarily set minimum prices on farm products. Just like Russia's Gosplan, the approach failed miserably. So the government simply established "above-equilibrium" price supports for farm products. That meant the government ignored real-world prices and paid farmers an inflated price. Another major blunder.

Farmers began producing a surplus because the government had promised to pay them the higher price *no matter how much they produced*. With the extra government money, they could cultivate more land and produce larger yields. Meat growers, milk producers, and poultry farmers could likewise improve their operations so they could all produce more.

Not surprisingly, huge surpluses were created. In the real world of economics, product surpluses send out market signals for prices to fall. Consumers purchase the excess at a reduced price, and the market quickly levels out. But the government was obligated to pay farmers the above-equilibrium price, as well as the costs for transportation and storage. Meanwhile, the surpluses continued to grow.

The government was then forced to raise taxes to cover their ignorance. Administrative costs skyrocketed as the government endeavored to manipulate the programs. Farmers formed lobby groups to protect the good thing they had going. The marginal costs of surplus production far exceeded the marginal benefit to consumers, since prices couldn't be lowered. As a result, consumers were forced to pay a premium for the products even though the surplus was going to waste.

That, in turn, made our agricultural markets very attractive to foreign producers, who took advantage of the above-equilibrium prices. To avert disaster, the US government had to scramble to impose import barriers, tariffs, and trade quotas.

Then the Roosevelt Gosplan architects came up with a brilliant idea. They could save millions in program costs if farmers stopped producing so much. But the government couldn't simply stop the craziness and let the free-enterprise system straighten out the mess. Farmers would have been furious, and FDR couldn't run the risk of losing those precious votes. So his architects decided to pay farmers *not* to grow their crops (or raise their livestock). In exchange for guaranteed payments based on the past year's yield price, farmers had to limit the number of acres they planted of a certain crop. That was referred to as an *acreage allotment*.

After estimating consumer demand, government bean counters calculated how many acres had to be planted to meet their estimate. Then the total acreage had to be apportioned among states, counties, and individual farms. The government could never get the calculations right. Reducing the farm acreage failed to proportionately reduce production as intended. Some farmers included their worst land in the allotment and saved their best land for growing more crops and making even more money to reinvest in better seed, enriched fertilizers, and the newest farm equipment.

Farmers who declined the subsidies bought up more acreage and planted more crops in anticipation of benefiting from the artificially increased prices. And all this time, the surpluses continued to escalate, and farmers were raking in boatloads of cash for not growing crops or raising livestock. That old Texas hog farmer was happily pocketing the profits for not raising hogs and for not feeding corn that was not being grown to hogs that were not being raised.

Oh, what's to be done? Governments that insist on ignoring basic economic principles like supply and demand usually end up in a very tangled web, thinking they can manipulate people to advance their own interests. But eventually they step on the neck of the goose that has been laying all the golden eggs.

Manipulating Demand

When it finally dawned on Roosevelt's Gosplan architects that they couldn't successfully manipulate the supply side of the equation, they came up with another brilliant idea. If they could get rid of the surpluses and increase demand for the remaining supply, people would gladly pay a higher price for the scarce products. If the planners played it right, they could dispose of the surpluses and buy even more votes by promising subsidies to new groups of voters.

On April 20, 1939, the Roosevelt administration unveiled the Food Stamps Plan (commonly referred to as the Food Stamps Program), which was designed to reduce the farm surplus. Food-stamp recipients could purchase $1.50 worth of food with $1.00 worth of food stamps. What a deal. Of course folks will vote for someone who supplies them with free food.

Since then, Congress has frequently enhanced the Food Stamp Program.[3] In the sixties, the government expanded the program to every state and increased accessibility. Eventually, Electronic Benefit Transfer (EBT) cards were distributed to food-stamp recipients, but the system has been rife with fraud and abuse. Colorado recipients, for example, were reportedly caught swiping their EBT cards at ATM machines for fast cash and then purchasing marijuana with taxpayer money.[4]

In 2008, the Food Stamp Program was given a more user-friendly name—the Supplemental Nutrition Assistance Program, or SNAP[5]—and yet another subsidy was approved. The USDA hailed SNAP as "the largest program in the domestic hunger safety net."[6] As of 2014, the program was supplying free food to more than forty-six million socially dependent recipients per month.[7]

In addition to the Food Stamp Program, the government dreamed up other creative ways to dispense with the crop surpluses. The school lunch program was established in 1946 "to safeguard the health and well-being of the nation's children and to encourage the domestic consumption of nutritious agricultural commodities."[8]

According to the official story, the "agricultural commodities" were donated, but that's just a sweet way of saying they actually came from commandeered tax monies used to buy the votes of farmers who raised the commodities.[9]

The next ingenious idea was to feed the world from America's abundant agricultural surplus. The Agricultural Trade Development and Assistance Act of 1954 and the international Food for Peace program would provide "a means whereby surplus agricultural commodities in excess of the usual marketings of such commodities may be sold." At the signing ceremony, President Eisenhower stated that the law would "lay the basis for a permanent expansion of our exports of agricultural products, with lasting benefits to ourselves and peoples in other lands."[10] US farmers were only too happy to embrace any legislation that would bring economic stability to the farming industry by maximizing the distribution of their agricultural products.

In a stump speech six years later, John F. Kennedy declared, "I don't regard the problem of agricultural surplus as a problem. I regard it as an opportunity to use it imaginatively, not only for our own people, but for people all around the world."[11] Only a grinch would condemn such generosity. But the truth, as always, was safely hidden behind feel-good rhetoric and idealistic political spin.

Recent endeavors to enhance the demand for surplus crops have included the production of gasohol—a gasoline-ethanol blend—and biodiesel. As politicians have discovered, creating a demand for surplus products and heavily subsidizing that demand has worked even better in procuring votes than supply-side subsidies. Is it any wonder that the federal government has vehemently opposed private-sector energy research and development?

I can hear the voice of reason hollering, "Stop, stop, STOP all this tragic foolishness!" Why are taxpayers shelling out billions of dollars each year for farm programs, just for the privilege of paying twice the normal market price for milk? The answer is obvious: so politicians can secure votes to maintain their greedy power and control.

The solution to the government's tangled farm-policy web is simple. It's called free enterprise. The Gosplan gurus don't need to keep trying—and failing—to get it all right with acreage allotments, long division, and stubby pencils. Here's a brilliant idea: let the agricultural folks decide for themselves what they want to grow and to whom they wish to sell their products, and let the politicians earn their votes through creativity, expansion, and production rather than manipulation, taxation, and redistribution. Family farmers are very intelligent, caring, and industrious busi-nessmen. (I should know, since I grew up in Idaho and married the prettiest and smartest farmer's daughter I could find.)

The free market will provide all the information farmers need to make good decisions as they freely choose what's best for them. And all those free choices in the marketplace will make even more people better off.

Farming in the Twenty-First Century

From the 1930s to the early 1990s, farm families had dwindled to less than 1.5 percent of the US population.[12] Many had sold their land to large corporate agri-businesses and left farming behind. Urban representatives in Congress now had a ten-to-one majority over rural representatives.

By 1996, the political tide had turned, and politicians now believed it was time to wean farmers off their subsidies and stop paying above-equilibrium crop prices. In real-world language that means it was no longer expedient for politicians to buy farmers' votes to get elected. The course correction *almost* sounded like a return to free-enterprise principles and freedom of choice.

To ease the transition, Congress passed the Freedom to Farm Act, which radi-cally overhauled the previous seventy years of farming. The plan set up declining annual crop payments for seven years at a cost of $37 billion. But there was a fly in the ointment. The government agreed to pay farmers based on *previous* commod-ity prices and production levels, *regardless of current economic conditions or need.* So much for reform.

By 1999, the reform measures completely fell apart, and the government passed an even more expensive emergency-aid package of farm subsidies. In 2002, the Farm Security and Rural Investment Act was established, setting aside even more money for automatic emergency farm aid. You've probably guessed it. The payments were guaranteed, *whether or not there was an emergency*. Rather than decreasing the payments over time and weaning farmers off the subsidies, the payments became a *permanent* subsidy.

So, what happened to all the farm families whose votes were so essential to keep FDR in office? The families have all but vanished, and gigantic agricultural corporations have taken their place. Ironically, they are now receiving the government subsidies previously granted to family farms. Apparently agribusiness is now considered an endangered way of life that must be protected at all costs.

The family farm has become a rare commodity in the twenty-first century. Some families walked away after generations of farming because they were sick and tired of government interference. Others were lured away by new job opportunities. Still others began to buy up their neighbors' acreage to increase their government subsidies. Pretty soon, investors formed corporations and purchased lots of fertile acreage to qualify for the subsidies. As competition drove land prices higher, small farmers seized the opportunity to sell their farms.

Land prices also got a boost from Earl Butz, the secretary of agriculture under presidents Nixon and Ford. Butz abolished programs that paid farmers not to plant crops or raise livestock and encouraged farmers to plant crops "from fence row to fence row" and increase their crop yields.[13] His exuberant message to the agricultural community was "Get big or get out."[14]

The giant agribusinesses saw the new policies as a green light to increase in size and scope. Land prices surged, and more small farmers seized the opportunity to sell their farms and walk away with a profit. But the redistribution camp couldn't tolerate a return to free enterprise, so they gutted the Freedom to Farm Act and reinstituted direct payments and emergency farm aid. As a result, farm controls became even more deeply entrenched.

The government eventually realized that billions in profits could be reaped if agribusinesses owned and developed the land. The corporations would continue benefiting from government subsidies and price controls, and the government would benefit from massive tax revenues.

Politicians have also found it advantageous to collaborate with agricultural corporations. Through political action committees (PACs), agribusinesses transfer wealth to special-interest groups by lobbying legislators to vote for programs that will benefit them. Once the votes are secured, the PACs channel political contributions to those legislators. Lobbying is just one way agribusinesses can receive a generous assortment of government benefits. But what most busy taxpayers don't know is that agribusinesses get paid millions of taxpayer dollars each year from government agricultural programs to lobby Congress.

Another political scheme called *logrolling* enables legislators to swap votes. For example, one senator may agree to vote for a subsidy that benefits sugar-beet growers in another senator's state. The senator from the sugar-beet state then returns the favor by voting for a measure that benefits the first senator's state, such as a school lunch program. The vote swap may have more to do with financing a reelection campaign than benefiting a legislator's constituents.

These politically opportunistic practices help explain why farm subsidies and other government programs are so deeply entrenched in our culture.

The collaboration between the government and agricultural corporations is an ingenious way to redistribute wealth, but the simple fact remains that the erosion of free enterprise will only make us poorer as a nation.

PART **3**

A NEW
ECONOMIC
PARADIGM

ENVISIONING A WORLD
OF ABUNDANCE

enowned British author C. S. Lewis routinely walked about ten miles a day while he was teaching at Oxford University. He used that time to contemplate, dream, and imagine. *Suppose* there were a world like Narnia. *Suppose* it had talking animals in it. Lewis referred to his musings as "supposals."[1] A story about a talking lion, a witch, and kids entering another world through a wardrobe was a supposal.

As a worldwide observer, I've done a little supposin' of my own. I've noticed that the earth's inhabitants have not only accomplished some incredible feats, but they've also produced some very sad results. Some people have used the contents of their market baskets to make others better off, abundantly blessing present and future generations. Others have squandered their possessions or misused the contents of their market baskets, leaving others worse off.

In the world today, the unquestioning acceptance of the scarcity, choice, and cost trilogy has promoted an expectation of absolute insufficiency and lack. That acceptance, in my view, has led to fallacious conclusions regarding reality. It's high time we challenge the groupthink regarding scarcity and shake up the status quo with a little supposin' of our own.

- Suppose our expectation of scarcity, insufficiency, and lack was completely
  wrong headed?

- Suppose that scarcity wasn't the true condition of our world today, and our resources weren't as hopelessly limited or depleted as we imagine them to be?
- Suppose that instead of spending our time and effort choosing between alternatives in a world of scarce resources, we used our intelligence, creativity, and energy to discover a world of *abundance*?
- Suppose we found ways to tap into new resources to meet our needs and invented new ways to harness and use the resources already available to us?
- Suppose we used the contents of our market baskets to make everyone better off rather than advancing our own selfish interests?

What would happen if we embraced an economic model based on the concept of *abundance* rather than scarcity? The world, I suspect, would be a radically better place in which to live.

When I was a small boy, my mom used to read me a story about young John D. Rockefeller and how he went to his neighboring state of Pennsylvania to check out a new industrial discovery called oil.[2] The area farmers cursed the black goop that oozed up to the surface because it interfered with their farming. While inspecting a field where the oil had surfaced and formed a sticky, black pond, John and his partner found it necessary to cross a rickety wooden bridge. John was halfway across the bridge when a plank broke and he plummeted into the oily slush below. Covered with oil from head to foot, John scrambled out of the sludge onto solid ground.

Whereupon his partner wryly stated, "I see that you have plunged into this oil business head over heels."

Rockefeller not only established an oil refinery near that site but also went on to discover and invent multiple uses for oil. Eventually he became president of the Standard Oil Company and, at that time, the wealthiest man in the world.

Who said that oil could be used as an energy source?

Who discovered that oil could be refined to produce the fuel that powers our cars and heats our homes?

Who figured out that electricity could be used to light our homes and operate countless devices?

Who figured out that water, sun, and wind could be harnessed to supply energy?

Who determined that a process called hydraulic fracturing, or fracking, would uncover vast new sources of energy?

What other great discovery or invention is just around the corner that could change our world for the better?

I have no earthly idea, but one thing I do know with certainty: if we so completely buy into the notion of shortage, depletion, and zero-sum economics that we fail to envision and pursue a universe of possibilities, we'll ultimately be the losers.

Just Imagine …

When I was a freshman in college in 1960, Dr. Maxwell Maltz published *Psycho-Cybernetics: A New Way to Get More Living out of Life.* He claimed that imagination activates and guides our "success mechanism."[3] We may live our lives in an imperfect world, but the doors of opportunity aren't all shut. New frontiers are out there just waiting to be discovered. Imagination, Maltz argued, can essentially determine what we become because it gives us the courage to bet on our ideas, calculate the risks, and act on our visions and dreams.

When I first read Maltz's book, I thought, *Well, sure, how would new inventions ever happen unless someone first had an idea, became convinced of the possibilities, and then risked translating that vision into reality?* Without imagination, pendulum clocks, steam engines, cameras, zippers, Velcro, and even peanut butter would never have been invented.

But the scary part of this proposition is that imagination is entirely under our control. We can imagine a world filled with good and beautiful things and envision scenarios of discovery and abundance, or we can allow ourselves to imagine bad or ugly things and a world of scarcity and depletion.

If we envision a world of scarcity and depletion, we'll be tempted to hoard, covet, and redistribute what others possess to give ourselves an advantage. That kind of focus squelches invention and ingenuity and encourages greed, entitlement, and selfish expansionism. It's a closed economy, a zero-sum game in which we must strategize to take our "fair share" of what presently exists.

I have come to believe that the doctrine of scarcity promotes bondage, and the doctrine of abundance promotes freedom. As we saw earlier, one of the weaknesses of the redistribution system created by Marx, Engels, and Lenin was that they saw the wealth of the tsars as merely a pile of "stuff." They figured that if they could get their hands on the golden egg, they would be able to redistribute it according to their dictates of equity and fairness, and everyone would live happily ever after. But their system was inherently flawed because it failed to factor growth, ingenuity, investment, positive incentive, rewards, enterprise, discovery, or sustainability in the equation. It never dawned on them that production generates wealth, and wealth in the form of income pays the bills.

Years later, when the tsar's golden egg was used up, the Communists had only one sustainability option: they resorted to invading, raping, and pillaging their neighbors to pay the bills. They became what they had imagined themselves to be.

When I read Maltz's statement that our imaginations will essentially determine what we become, that line of reasoning struck a chord of truth with me because my dad used to caution his three creative sons, "Be alert, because you will ultimately become what you think about all day long."

In our home as boys, we were never allowed to say "I can't." The "shortage" excuse wasn't an option. If we said "I can't" to avoid doing what we were told to do, we were given the exercise of figuring out *ten* ways, instead of *one* way, to accomplish the task.

I remember my brother Bill walking through the house one day with his canvas tennis shoe flapping in the breeze. Our dad instructed him to tie his shoe so that the tongue wouldn't flap and the shoe would stay on properly.

Bill made the mistake of saying "I can't," because he had lost the shoestring.

Thereupon, my dad sat him down, and they figured out ten different ways to bind up the shoe to keep the tongue from flapping. They came up with string, wire, bailing twine, an old piece of electric extension cord, and six other ingenious ways to secure the shoe.

Our dad would always conclude such exercises by telling us that it would be far easier if we simply found one good method to take care of the problem in the first place rather than saying "I can't" and then having to figure out ten different solutions.

I learned early in life that an "I can't" attitude can become an excuse for not even trying to use creativity and ingenuity to solve problems. The focus of our imaginations ultimately determines what we become. If we aren't careful, our perception of scarcity and depletion can become a self-fulfilling prophecy.

The Trilogy of Abundance, Choice, and Accomplishment

Suppose we adopted a new economic paradigm of *abundance*, *choice*, and *accomplishment* in lieu of the traditional paradigm of scarcity, choice, and cost? According to the traditional view we discussed earlier, every resource is presumed to be scarce when it has at least two alternative uses. Choosing one alternative means forfeiting the next highest alternative and incurring a lost-opportunity cost, which represents the value of that alternative.

But suppose we had an abundance of resources that eliminated, or at least minimized, the lost-opportunity cost of our choices? We'd experience a whole new paradigm.

Some things wouldn't change, of course. We'd still need to make choices, since life will always be filled with alternatives. We'd still need to figure out *what* to produce from our resources and *who* would produce and distribute the resulting goods and services. We would still need to determine *how* and *for whom* the goods and services should be produced. Each of these aspects would require our creativity, our wills, and our ability to choose.

What *would* change, however, is the fundamental basis of our decisions. What if instead of believing the *inaccurate* reality of the scarcity model, we embraced the *accurate* reality that abundance is possible? For one thing, we'd no longer fall into the trap of thinking that if we choose alternative A, we'll automatically forgo alternative B (the lost-opportunity cost). Instead of expending our energy and creativity trying to figure out how to live with scarcity and manage our limited resources, we could channel all of that energy and God-given creativity into discovering new ways to increase our supply and tap into new resources so that everyone would end up better off.

The scarcity model, for example, has convinced us that energy has become an endangered resource. As of 2013, our civilization reportedly ran on 21.5 terawatts of power,[4] and yet we really need to triple or quadruple that amount to meet the energy needs of the twenty-first century. But instead of discovering how to increase our energy supply, we spend all of our time worrying about how to live with less power and arguing over who will control it. We consider selling energy credits to the highest bidders and passing laws to limit production and consumption. We even discuss ways to decrease demand through population control. All of these so-called solutions to the problem of limited supply are based on our shared belief in deficiency and inadequacy.

Wouldn't it make more sense to base our choices on the possibility of abundance?

When I consider the paradigm of abundance, choice, and accomplishment, George Washington Carver comes to mind.[5] Carver was born into slavery in Missouri around 1861, but by 1865, slavery had been abolished, opening the door for Carver to pursue an education. He had an unquenchable passion for learning and eventually became an inventor, scientist, botanist, and professor at Tuskegee University, where he worked for forty-seven years. The South had become a one-crop cotton culture during that time. The soil had become depleted, and the boll weevil was spoiling any cotton that could be grown. Carver creatively took up the challenge of introducing alternative crops that would pump needed nutrition into the ground and into the farm families' tummies. Instead of basing his choices on a paradigm of poverty, he pursued a paradigm of plenty.

Mr. Carver started experimenting with the lowly peanut, inventing 300 alternative uses, including cosmetics, dyes, paints, plastics, gasoline, and nitroglycerin. He also came up with 105 recipes using peanuts. Sweet potatoes and soybeans then caught his attention. Products from the sweet potato alone included wood fillers, dyes, breakfast foods, molasses, glue for library books, vinegars, coffee, after-dinner mints, lemon drops, and orange drops.

Carver told Raleigh Merritt, one of his biographers, that he was merely scratching the surface of uses for the peanut and other resources. It was fortunate for Mr. Carver that no one from our generation was present to persuade him that the model of abundance, choice, and accomplishment was wrong-headed. I wonder how many more products and alternative uses Mr. Carver would have discovered had he lived another fifty years. Modern-day economists would have had a difficult time convincing him that we live in a world of scarcity and zero-sum economics.

In my work with Project C.U.R.E., I personally witnessed miracles of abundance. While I was in Nagorno-Karabakh, I saw devastation and scores of maimed victims. Constant bombing and hidden land mines had left people without arms or legs. Many victims needed physical rehabilitation and prosthetic limbs to be restored to health, so I promised the doctors and nurses that Project C.U.R.E. would help them establish a rehab facility in the city of Stepanakert and provide the necessary supplies.

When I returned to Denver, I discovered that we had sent all the rehabilitation equipment in our Project C.U.R.E. warehouse to a hospital in Turkey. What could we do? The time was quickly approaching when we had to ship the cargo of equipment to Yerevan, Armenia, and then transport it by land to Stepanakert.

Justin, the young man in charge of our Denver warehouse, and his crew began to pray for the people in Nagorno-Karabakh. They asked God to miraculously provide the needed rehabilitation equipment and prosthetic devices. Justin even posted the Karabakh inventory list on his warehouse desk as a reminder.

Then one day the warehouse crew was notified that a large truck would be arriving at our docks. The truck was loaded with assorted medical goods that a prominent medical company had donated to Project C.U.R.E. When the truck backed into the dock space, the driver hopped out and handed Justin the manifest.

"Jim, it was a miracle, an absolute miracle!" Justin told me later, with tears welling up in his eyes. "My helper, Jerry, and I just stood there. I had the delivery manifest in one hand and the Karabakh inventory list in my other hand. The two lists were almost identical.

"When we arrived at the warehouse this morning," he went on, "we didn't have any of the equipment we needed. Then within an hour, we had nearly everything on that inventory list. Now the rehab center in Karabakh will have the equipment they need, plus lots of other medical supplies they didn't expect. We've just been part of a miracle."

I've learned that I can afford to give abundantly because God's abundant resources are always available. The trilogy of abundance, choice, and accomplishment is an eternal economic principle that we can stake our lives on.

The Naughty Watchdog

What keeps us from embracing the paradigm of abundance, choice, and accomplishment? It's an immensely powerful emotion called fear. The role of fear, of course, is to warn us when we're in danger and keep us out of harm's way. That's a good thing. Without healthy fear, we might walk off the edge of a cliff or forget to look both ways before crossing a busy street.

The fear center in our brains, called the amygdala (ah-mig-dala), is a lot like a watchdog. In fact, I like to think of it as the *rottweiler of the brain*. As standard equipment in our brains, the amygdala is a warning system that remains on guard, scanning the horizon for threats to our safety and well-being. When triggered, it engages the fight-or-flight response that plays a crucial role in survival. It never slumbers or sleeps, and its bark sends instant messages to the heart, lungs, nerves, skin, eyes, ears, and memory chips in our brains, and even prepares our muscles for instant action.

The amygdala was born and bred to be the ultimate watchdog that beautifully alerts us to danger and ignites our fear mechanism to keep us alive. This rottweiler of the brain is always on the lookout for danger and will *always* find something to bark at.

Fear, however, can also prevent us from doing what's right or best. And that's *not* a good thing. Left to do what comes naturally, our watchdogs can become undisciplined and unruly, focusing all of their attention—and ours—on problems, problems, problems. When that happens, we tend to develop a fear-based view of life and make decisions from a standpoint of scarcity and depletion rather than abundance. The atmosphere can become more pessimistic than optimistic as a fear-based mind-set morphs into a full-time search for trouble.

What happens when we become incessantly preoccupied with scarcity and depletion?

- Our fear of scarcity can blind us to the good things that are happening in the world today, as well as the possibilities of future triumphs. When we lose a proper perspective regarding the good things we already possess, we tend to hoard and become stingy toward others.

- We abandon an attitude of gratitude and become acutely aware of what other people have in comparison to what we have. We're tempted to believe that others have more because they somehow took our share away from us.

- We think up ways to redistribute what others have so that those things can justifiably become our own. We may even become attracted to people we consider strong enough to take away things from the people who possess them and redistribute them to us.

- We begin to think we're entitled to more than we have, and we fear that we might end up with even less. We spend our time worrying about not having enough, even though we've never figured out just how much is enough.

- Our fear of scarcity and our preoccupation with perceived inequities shut down our creative problem-solving skills and drive us toward deeper dependency on government and other groups that offer to take care of us.

Every time our watchdogs bark, even at their own shadows, we can become paralyzed by fear. It's time to stop this goofy game and tell the naughty doggy "No!"

Suppose you could hush the rottweiler in your brain and ratchet down the fear to make room for hope and confidence in the possibility of abundance? After a bit of brainstorming, I've come up with a few ways you can tighten the leash on that watchdog of yours:

- Remember, an attitude of scarcity promotes bondage, but an attitude of abundance promotes freedom. The fear of scarcity can become a self-fulfilling prophecy if you allow it to control you.

- Limit the tsunami of negative media entering your conscious and subconscious mind. Just say "No, thank you." to 90 percent of the news.

- When you pay undue attention to your rottweiler, giving him a pet treat and a pat on the head whenever he barks, you're encouraging him to engage in more of the same fearmongering behavior. Quit rewarding your watchdog when he barks at his own shadow. Rather than encouraging him, command him to sit down and shut up.

- Train your watchdog to perceive that the people approaching you may be your best friends, not intruders or predators. Not all situations or circumstances are threats to your survival. They may actually be blessings of abundance in surprise.

- Dare to investigate and apply the concept of "my God will meet all your needs".

- Start deleting the negative, fear-based information stored on the memory chips of your amygdala and replace it with new, positive information based on sufficiency, abundance, and accomplishment. One way to do this is to choose daily to focus your thoughts on whatever is good, right, true, pure, lovely, and admirable.

The fear of scarcity is a universal problem, not just an American issue. I've observed the machinations of fear in cultures all over the world. But here's the *good news*: the disposition of the naughty watchdog can be altered. We can shed the old logic of the limited and embrace a new paradigm of abundance.

A quick look at history is a good place to start. History validates the fact that things aren't as bad as we've been made to believe. Real progress is happening right now where we live. It's fair to say that never before in history have living standards improved as dramatically as they have in the past century. Who would have thought a hundred years ago that even the poorest folks in America today would be enjoying such luxuries as indoor flush toilets, automobiles, telephones, and televisions? It's high time we take a second look at the abundance our culture presently enjoys and how rapidly things can change for the better.

A LOOK AT PROGRESS— PART 1

Suppose we engage in a brave experiment that will silence the continual yapping of our watchdogs and turn up the volume on some positive reports of progress in our world. We may not realize it, but thanks to the technological and cultural advancements of the modern era, we are, generally speaking, healthier, wealthier, and safer than any previous inhabitants on this old earth. As you adjust your mind-set to notice the abundance around you, you might even find yourself smiling for a change.

From Atoms to Exabytes

When I was eleven years old, Dwight D. Eisenhower ran against Adlai Stevenson for the presidency of the United States. I was so passionate about the general that I wore an "I Like Ike" button and made a poster for the campaign. I even wrote a poem in his honor. World War II was over, and I recall General Eisenhower assuring the American people that the technology used to develop the atom bomb could be harnessed for peaceful purposes.

He talked about nuclear power turning saltwater into freshwater that could be used to irrigate arable land around the world and transform it into a breadbasket for millions of hungry people. He also explained that the harnessed power of the atom could one day be safely used so that shortages of electricity would never occur again anywhere on the earth.

After his election, President Eisenhower spoke to the fledgling United Nations in 1953 and laid out the plan for his Atoms for Peace program:

> The United States pledges before you—and therefore before the world—its determination to help solve the fearful atomic dilemma—to devote its entire heart and mind to find the way by which the miraculous inventiveness of man shall not be dedicated to his death, but consecrated to his life.[1]

Unfortunately, imposed fear and political manipulation pretty much sabotaged President Eisenhower's dream. In the ensuing years, technological advances in atomic research lagged behind, but the knowledge base grew exponentially. The vision never faded, and now, for the first time, information and technology are catching up with our dreams and ambitions, not just in the area of atomic power (which we'll discuss in the next chapter), but in so many other areas of life.

Computer technology is one area in which technology has caught up with, and even surpassed, our wildest dreams. Google's executive chairman, Eric Schmidt, calculated that from the beginning of time until the year 2003, the human race created five exabytes of digital information. (An *exabyte* is one billion gigabytes, or a one followed by eighteen zeros.) By the year 2010, we were generating five exabytes of information every few days. And in the near future, humans are expected to produce five exabytes every ten minutes.[2]

On average, technologies are doubling in power every eighteen months to keep up with the exponential supply of knowledge and information. The prices for those technologies are also being slashed in half every eighteen months. Affordability continues to drive growth. Inventions based on today's technologies are usually outdated by the time they get to market. That's a marvelous thing.

Exciting developments have been taking place in the Silicon Valley. Gordon Moore's famous tech trend of cramming more and more components onto integrated circuits has paid off handsomely. As a result, computer processing power has doubled approximately every two years since the integrated circuit was invented in 1958, a phenomenon known as Moore's law.[3]

IBM is also developing breakthrough technologies by integrating electrical and optical devices on the same silicon chip. Instead of the old electrical signals, the new chips communicate with light signals. That effectively eliminates the historical problems of heat generation that have required vast amounts of energy for cooling and have limited computer speed.

According to conservative estimates, IBM's new chip design could increase a supercomputer's processing speed one thousandfold, from the present 2.6 petaflops to a full exaflop. (The rumor is *not* true, however, that IBM is becoming a "flophouse.") The new chip would enable computers to perform a quintillion operations per second.[4] Simply speaking, that's one thousand times faster than today's fastest supercomputers. And we used to marvel that the old horse-and-buggy computers could beat the Russian chess champion on a regular basis.

In 2009, Kevin Ashton wrote an article in the *RFID Journal* on the Internet of Things (IoT). In the article he stated that

> today's information technology is so dependent on data originated by people that our computers know more about ideas than things. If we had computers that knew everything there was to know about things— using data they gathered without any help from us—we would be able to track and count everything, and greatly reduce waste, loss and cost. We would know when things needed replacing, repairing or recalling, and whether they were fresh or past their best. … The Internet of Things has the potential to change the world, just as the Internet did. Maybe even more so.[5]

The Internet of Things (IoT) is based on the idea that if all the objects we use in daily life were equipped with a minuscule identifying device or machine-readable identifier, computers could follow, manage, and inventory them. It could completely transform how we live and conduct business. For example, reorders would be created and activated automatically, and businesses would no longer run out of stock. Machines could also communicate via a network of sensors and receptors to identify and perform specific maintenance and repair tasks.

The Internet of Things is already in operation, with nearly 30 billion connected devices.[6] Transponders are just one example of the types of devices currently in use. These devices perform a wide variety of communications, monitoring, and signaling functions, including monitoring organ function; tracking animal health, behavior, and location; reporting mechanical and safety information for vehicles; and providing essential communication support for firefighters and rescue personnel. The Federal Trade Commission (FTC) projects that by 2020, 50 billion devices will be wirelessly connected to the Internet of Things.[7]

Another important player in the IoT is Vint Cerf, a real, honest-to-goodness father of the Internet. At MCI he engineered and managed the first commercial e-mail service, and he also served as chairman with the Internet Corporation for Assigned Names and Numbers (ICANN). Cerf has now been assigned to design a program called Ipv6. Suppose each person in the world had somewhere between one and five thousand things that needed to be identified. It would currently take 45,000 billion IP addresses on the Internet of Things to handle the communication network. But the new Ipv6 program protocols will be able to handle 340 trillion, trillion, trillion unique IP addresses, which breaks down to about 50,000 trillion, trillion unique addresses per individual. Junior would no longer lose his laptop computer with his homework assignment on it. Come to think of it, no one would be able to steal his laptop either.

Dr. Cerf says that the Ipv6 Internet of Things "holds the promise for reinventing almost every industry. How we manufacture, how we control our environment, and how we distribute, use, and recycle resources."[8]

Energy Bust or Boom?

My international travels have included most of the oil-cartel countries of the world. Whenever I've boarded a plane to leave one of these countries, I've found myself looking forward to a postpetroleum world economy and wondering why we've remained so long in the pitiful position of oil dependency. These oil-rich countries have contributed no ingenious inventions to the world; no scientific or industrial breakthroughs; no brilliant economic systems; no art, literature, or music—just boatloads of oil.

Notice that I said "oil dependency." The United States is currently awash in oil and gas. There is no scarcity. However, the politics of oil *availability* is a road with many potholes and devious curves. Yet as history and economics bear out, potholes eventually get filled, and annoying curves get straightened out. My bet here is on change.

Maury Harris, a chief US economist, remarked a few years ago that North Dakota could join OPEC.[9] From 2013 to 2014, oil production in North Dakota shot from nearly 800,000 barrels a day to more than a million, and by 2017, production is expected to hit 1.5 million barrels.[10] The boom in fracking (hydraulic fracturing) has ignited economic growth with a corresponding reduction in unemployment. According to the Bureau of Labor Statistics, North Dakota's unemployment rate in January of 2015 was the lowest in the country at 2.8 percent, compared to 5.7 percent nationally.[11] Williston, North Dakota, the epicenter of the fracking boom, has enjoyed an unemployment rate as low as .7 percent in 2012, and as of January 2015, the rate was still well below the national average at 1.6 percent.[12]

According to economist Ed Yardeni,

The Fracking Dividend … narrowed [the] US petroleum trade deficit from a … peak of $359 billion … during January 2012 to $182 billion during November 2013. [A further reduction] would provide a big dividend to real GDP growth, as well as more purchasing power for Americans. Building the infrastructure to export crude oil would be another benefit, especially for capital goods manufacturers.[13]

Exporting our own oil also "helped cut the US trade deficit to a four-year low [in 2014]. Petroleum product exports climbed to an all-time high of $13.3 billion. Meanwhile, crude imports declined to $28.5 billion, the lowest since November 2010. The petroleum deficit thus shrank to $15.2 billion in November, the lowest since May 2009."[14]

Although a "supply glut" and a decrease in global demand for oil is expected to continue in 2016,[15] it's abundantly clear that neither oil nor natural gas is scarce. In fact, the US Energy Information Administration projects strong growth in oil and natural gas production through 2020 and steady production through at least 2040.[16]

So why aren't we allowed to use our own inexpensive energy resources? As is so often the case, the answer is politics. Politics and politicians have a great propensity for erecting roadblocks that curb successful ventures and suffocate free enterprise. But economics eventually trumps politics. If the oil industry is thwarted in utilizing the rich resources of the United States and is forced instead to export crude oil and natural gas to shrink the trade deficit, then more than likely, those entrepreneurs will tap into the vast cache of information we've been accumulating and construct a detour around this politically generated problem.

Another area of energy exploration and development that is showing some promise is biofuels. Oil giant ExxonMobil announced in 2009 that the company would commit $600 million over the following six years to develop a whole new generation of biofuels.[17] Most of us remember earlier unsuccessful attempts to create ethanol gasoline out of corn. That didn't work out so well. But Exxon decided to team up with DNA superscientist Craig Venter to manufacture inexpensive fuels.

Instead of extracting oil from holes drilled in the earth, they planned to grow a new type of algae that can take carbon dioxide and plentiful ocean water and create oil or any other kind of fuel that will please the market. The designer algae excrete oil that is then manufactured into biofuel. In 2009, Venter sailed his *Sorcerer II* yacht around the world gathering samples of algae to process through his DNA sequencing apparatus. During that expedition, he collected more than forty million different genes that could be modified in the future to manufacture a large variety of biofuels.[18] All the algae need to produce the oil is sunlight, carbon dioxide, and seawater.[19] As of 2013, Venter's team at Synthetic Genomics report that in four years "considerable knowledge" was gained about developing algae into biofuel, but so far, algae has proved to be "too expensive to compete with fossil fuels."[20]

Exponential knowledge and information growth in such areas as biotechnology make it possible to harness the necessary resources to make everyone better off.

The Wet Stuff

Seventy percent of the earth's surface is covered with water … real deep pools of water. We don't have a shortage of water despite what the environmentalists and politicians claim. The issue has never been the global scarcity of water; it's always been about *global accessibility*. Selfish control and manipulation are the issue. The politics of scarcity and fear over perceived scarcity are the issue. The wars that are fought and the people who are slaughtered over presumably scarce resources are the issue.

I believe it puts a smile on God's face when we discover the insights and wisdom he has already shared with us. We honor and worship him when we desire to imitate his creativity. And the more we learn about this world he created, the more our knowledge grows. Future discoveries await us if we'll just put our bountiful innovation and creativity to work.

Let's look at some exciting technological advances with water. For twenty-five years, I served on a water and sanitation board in Colorado. I don't know that I had much to offer, but I certainly learned a lot about water. I discovered, for example, that ski areas could use river water to make artificial snow, but citizens were allowed to water their yards only two nights a week. I learned that Colorado municipalities were refused access to mountain-snow runoff, but California, Las Vegas, and New Mexico could use the same water to mist large downtown areas to keep the atmosphere pleasantly cool for customers. I learned that districts could arbitrarily ration water usage on a short-term basis and then enhance their revenues by raising utility rates because they weren't selling as many gallons of water. Oh, there was so much to learn about water, water rights, and water usage.

Fortunately I also heard some very positive and exciting news about water. A gifted inventor named Dean Kamen, who was concerned about worldwide access to safe drinking water and sterile water for medical use, developed the Slingshot.[21] Named for David's famous encounter with the giant Goliath, this simple method of producing sterile water uses vapor compression distillation and requires no filters. The device is about the size of a small apartment-sized refrigerator, with a power cord, an intake hose, and an outflow hose. It produces approximately 250 gallons of 100 percent pure water per day. That's enough pure water for the daily cooking, drinking, and hygiene needs of one hundred people, and it uses less than one kilowatt of power. Powering the device is the Stirling engine, another invention of Kamen's, which is designed to burn almost anything, including cow dung, and runs maintenance free for at least five years.

Kamen designed his Slingshot with the intention of transforming 97 percent of the earth's nonpotable (unusable) water into pure water that is readily and inexpensively available for consumption. As of 2009, each Slingshot cost Kamen's company more than one hundred thousand dollars to assemble, but by mass-producing the device, Kamen hopes to reduce the cost to two thousand dollars, which would enable the developing world to benefit from the technology.

Another inventor, Michael Pritchard, found it repulsive that loads and loads of bottled water are distributed in emergency situations.[22] So he developed probably the best hand-pumped water filters on the market. Until Pritchard's Lifesaver bottle came along, filters with membrane pores as tiny as two hundred nanometers were the benchmark. Such filters capture most bacteria, but the considerably smaller viruses still slip through.

Pritchard developed membranes with pores only fifteen nanometers wide that remove everything, including bacteria, viruses, cysts, fungi, parasites, and other water pathogens. One of Pritchard's filters cleans more than fifteen hundred gallons of water (four to six thousand liters) and then safely shuts itself down.[23] A five-gallon container equipped with a proper filter can supply enough clean water for a family of four for three years, and it costs only half a penny per day.[24]

A new era of molecular manufacturing is also being applied to the universal challenge of desalinating seawater. Both IBM and Central Glass, a Tokyo-based company, have recently developed a technology for removing both salt and arsenic from ocean water.[25] Since we have abundant supplies of hydrogen and oxygen—H_2O—many scientists predict that inexpensive methods of water purification will soon be available to meet the pressing needs for safe and sustainable drinking water.

While we're on the subject of water, let's look at the area of sanitation. The Environmental Protection Agency (EPA) estimates that more than one trillion gallons of water leak from US homes each year.[26] That's more than all the water used in Los Angeles, Miami, and Chicago combined. If you were to dump a gallon of water each second nonstop, it would take thirty-two thousand years (longer than all recorded history) to dump a trillion gallons. Toilets are the biggest water wasters. So it's time to dump the toilet.

To address this problem, the Bill and Melinda Gates Foundation offered $1.5 million in grants to researchers around the world to come up with more cost-efficient and environmentally friendly solutions.[27] Duke University worked to develop a technique in which "water is heated under pressure and then oxygen is added to burn up human waste."[28] Using another method, the University of Singapore sought to develop a toilet that "uses biochar to dry and combust feces [and] extract water from urine by boiling it under pressure. The system [would] recover highly purified water."[29] The Gates have recently backed a waterless design called the Nano

Membrane Toilet that has been approved for field testing later in 2016.[30] Consider for a moment how much we could save on the present cost of fresh water used for sanitation, to say nothing of the high cost of operating sewer lines and sanitation plants everywhere.

Other groups of researchers have been working to convert human waste into electricity using a variety of methods.[31] Energy generated from the waste will not only power your toilet one day but will also charge your cell phone and power your lights. The goal is to reduce operational costs to less than five cents per day so that underdeveloped countries can take advantage of the technologies.[32]

When bright people channel their energy and creativity into solving problems, everyone ends up better off. Supposin' that from now on we refuse to let the peddlers of gloom and doom blind our minds to the possibilities of abundance all around us.

A LOOK AT PROGRESS— PART 2

I hope this glimpse at progress is beginning to open your eyes and mind to the possibility of a world of abundance. I must admit I had an absolute hoot researching the prodigious discoveries and inventions taking place all around us.

The progress we've just explored has everything to do with cultural economics. On the economic side, we've witnessed the exponential growth in knowledge and technology that has produced amazing breakthroughs. And on the cultural side, we've seen how those breakthroughs are transforming the lives and behavior of people around the world. Enormously powerful changes are taking place at the intersection of culture and economics. It's an exciting time to be alive.

Before we conclude our little experiment, let's explore a few more examples of recent progress.

A 3-D World

While traveling in India and other parts of Asia, I marveled at the exquisite pieces of art produced with computer-controlled lasers, cutters, and shapers. These precision instruments trimmed away (or subtracted) unwanted portions of some material—wood, steel, glass, jade, precious metals, ice, or coconut shells—to create a breathtaking artistic masterpiece.[1] This process, called computer numerical controlled machining (CNC), amazed me.

But when I first heard about the 3-D printer, I was hooked. *How in the world can they do that?* I wondered. In 1986, Charles Hull of 3D Systems patented the first generation of digital-fabrication technology (3-D printing or stereolithography).[2] In recent years, Carl Bass, Autodesk's CEO and software designer, has successfully produced the latest generation of 3-D technology.[3] This technology makes it possible to add material in the fabrication process—additive manufacturing (AM)—rather than just whittling away what isn't needed. Now the computer instructs the printer to deposit successive layers of materials, such as steel, glass, plastic, or some new composite material to form a precise computer-designed shape.[4]

Soon 3-D printers will be found as readily in the shop, office, or home as the standard ink-jet printers of today. When that happens, fabrication and manufacturing will change forever. Whenever something breaks, you'll be able to fabricate the spare part on your own 3-D printer. You'll either design your own replacement part or download instructions from the Internet that will instruct your 3-D printer to produce the desired product.

I'm an antique-car buff, and I can hardly wait to get my hands on my first 3-D printer. Can you imagine being able to simply make your own missing carburetor part or piece of trim with your computer and 3-D printer? You'll be able to let your creativity run wild. I suppose an astronaut could even remake a broken part for his spaceship in midflight. And the prototypes of new inventions will be made in a fraction of the time it now takes.

This technology has begun to make its mark in the medical industry as well. Researchers are not only fabricating lifelike prosthetics with 3-D printers, but they're also designing vital body organs that can replace damaged or failing organs.[5] One day this technology may eliminate the need for organ transplants, as well as the associated risks. In another medical application, doctors replicated a human skull on their 3-D printer to replace a patient's crushed skull. In 2015, doctors also used a 3-D printer to "reconstruct" the skull of a Chinese toddler suffering from hydrocephalus. The new skull was then implanted using titanium mesh.[6] Remarkable!

One unique function of the 3-D printer is the ability to create new materials by weaving and embedding unique substances into fabrics to decrease weight but increase strength, flexibility, and resistance to outside elements.[7]

The possibilities for this revolutionary technology are seemingly endless.

Making Everyone Better Off

When I started traveling in Africa in the early 1980s, Telex machines offered the only international electronic connection to countries like Zimbabwe. Other than that, I had to rely on air-mail service, which required about ten days to communicate back and forth. It would take forever just to make travel arrangements and hotel reservations, confirm who would be at the airport to meet me, and handle any other arrangements.

So when the fax machine was introduced, I thought I'd arrived in heaven. Eventually the marvelous invention of e-mail followed. In such a short time, it seems, many African countries have gained access to Internet and wireless technologies. And since the technology is wireless, they've been spared the arduous task of installing telephone lines, thereby saving millions of dollars.

With the inception of microlending programs in sub-Saharan Africa, the number of mobile-phone subscribers climbed steadily from 16 million in 2000 to 376 million in 2008.[8] According to the International Telecommunication Union (ITU), as of May 2014, there were 629 million cell phone subscribers across the continent.[9] By 2015, that number reached 910 million subscribers and is projected to continue growing through 2020.[10] Now a typical African businessman with a cell phone has better information and communication capabilities than the president of the United States did in the 1980s. And if that businessman has Google and a smartphone, he has better information than the president did just fifteen years ago.

When Anna Marie and I visited Nairobi, Kenya, in January of 1994, we were invited to tour a coffee plantation outside Nakuru. Alfred, the plantation foreman, wanted to show us the plantation school. Inside each classroom was a chalkboard on the front wall and crude writing desks for up to forty-five students. No textbooks, curriculum, or reference books were available at the school, so the headmaster had to deliver the lesson materials to teachers every morning before classes began.

Students had to supply their own pens, pencils, and paper for homework assignments. When we asked where they got their supplies, they said that since they had no money for such things, they collected windblown paper scraps along the fencerows as they walked to and from school.

After returning home, Anna Marie organized the students and parents at her school in Evergreen, Colorado, and they shipped thousands of pounds of encyclopedias, noncultural library books, maps, and school supplies to the plantation school. We later found out that when the encyclopedias arrived, the teachers took them home and read them by the light of their cooking fires at night. That was in 1994.

Today those teachers aren't waiting for the headmaster to hand out lesson materials before class. They aren't even waiting for encyclopedias to arrive from Evergreen, Colorado. They now have wireless access to information that wasn't even available to Harvard University or the president of the United States a few years ago.

Very soon the entire world will have the technological advantages that only the affluent have been able to enjoy. Millions of people who have never before had access to the Internet or shared information will be coming online via computers and smartphones. They are a brand-new world market. Additionally, their contribution to global intelligence will result in new ideas, discoveries, inventions, and products.

Ignorance and scarcity bring poverty, but abundance and access to that abundance opens the door to freedom and opportunity.

Safe Nuclear Energy

I've saved my final example to honor one of my childhood heroes, president Dwight D. Eisenhower. One of the most effective contemporary organizations dedicated to carrying out Eisenhower's Atoms for Peace dream is TerraPower. Dr. Nathan Myhrvold, one of the brightest minds in the world today, and his colleagues at Terra-Power believe that "nuclear energy is the only proven generation source that can provide the large-scale, base load electricity needed to meet the world's growing energy demands."[11]

Generation 4 nuclear energy as a preferred, affordable, and safe alternative to fossil fuels and other energy sources has never been in a stronger position, and the energy industry is now seeing the potential benefits. Unfortunately, the continual bashing of nuclear energy over the past forty years nearly drowned out the triumphs and essentially brought construction of new facilities to a standstill. Whenever nuclear energy is mentioned, people tend to think of the Chernobyl disaster in 1986 or the reactor meltdown in Fukushima, Japan, in 2011. These catastrophes were indeed tragic, but the risks shouldn't prevent us from forging ahead with research and construction while making every effort to prevent future disasters. Despite these challenges and setbacks, however, nuclear-energy research and technology have made huge strides in recent years toward safer and more effective energy production.

In recent years, TerraPower and its founder, Bill Gates, began developing the traveling wave reactor (TWR), which Dr. Myhrvold claims is the world's most simplified passive fast-breeder reactor. TerraPower states the TWR cannot melt down, has no moving parts, and can shut down its own reactors without human help or interference.[12] Since the TWR doesn't require any nuclear enrichment, the risks and problems associated with handling spent fuel rods and storing nuclear waste are eliminated.

The hotter-burning Generation 4 technologies make a whole lot of sense. The TWR's small reactors can be designed to burn liquid fluoride thorium, which is four times more available than uranium and doesn't produce any long-lasting nuclear waste, since the waste is burned up. The liquid thorium could solve two problems at the same time by meeting the fuel needs of the TWR and burning up the existing supply of spent fuel rods. According to Dr. Myrhvold, "We could power the world for the next one thousand years just burning and disposing of the depleted uranium and spent fuel rods on today's stockpiles."[13]

TerraPower, Toshiba, and Westinghouse are also developing a Generation 4 small modular reactor called the SMR. The SMR, which is about the size of a refrigerator, can be manufactured, assembled, and sealed at a controlled assembly plant. These reactors are designed to operate for decades—some models have a sixty-year service life—and can safely store their own spent fuel. The size of the reactor makes it much easier to cool, and it also uses less fuel.[14]

Unlike conventional reactors, SMRs can be installed underground, which makes them less susceptible to earthquake damage, and when they reach the end of the line, they can be safely returned to the factory for dismantling and disposal. Apparently some models even come with their own sealed burial casks. Several SMRs are also designed to run on thorium rather than uranium.[15]

TerraPower, in collaboration with the Gates Foundation, wanted to invent a safe, cost-effective, and convenient power supply that can be built, buried, and forgotten. SMR technology could eventually be used not only in the United States but also in the developing world, where dams, windmills, and electric distribution grids are too time consuming and costly to erect. In fact, the Tennessee Valley Authority and the engineering company Babcock and Wilcox have reportedly teamed up to build the first SMR prototypes in Tennessee by 2022.[16]

When the peddlers of doom, gloom, and fear are hawking their wares at the top of their lungs, it's prime time for brave, forward-thinking, and creative folks to articulate a message of hope, possibility, and abundance. Thanks, President Eisenhower, for your dream to harness the power of the atom for peaceful purposes. I still like Ike.

By now I hope you've discovered that the birds of hope are everywhere. We desperately need to hear them sing. As Mark Twain once said, "There is no sadder sight than a young pessimist." But nothing is so refreshing and stabilizing as a maturing generation of optimists. Suppose we join those birds and sing a melody of hope and optimism.

23

THE POWER
OF GOODNESS

As I was writing about the astounding progress that's unfolding in our world today, some folks raised their eyebrows and asked, "Don't you see the mess the world is in?"

"Yes," I replied, "I understand that the world is in a mess, and civility is very fragile."

I've observed that mess firsthand in hot spots around the globe as a business consultant, humanitarian, and cultural economist. I've spent time in villages and homes in Africa, India, the old Soviet Union, Afghanistan, Iraq, Palestine, Laos, Cambodia, Burma (Myanmar), China, Pakistan, Brazil, Nagorno-Karabakh, North Korea, and many other locations. I've observed disturbing customs and traditions, bloody conflicts, and destructive economic practices, and I've asked government leaders and common citizens lots of questions. Many of these people became my personal friends and confided in me when I pushed for difficult answers to complex problems.

Almost everywhere I've traveled, I've wept over the terrible suffering of mothers and children, the horrific conditions people must endure day in and day out, and the utter cruelty of human beings toward one another. I've witnessed genocide, starvation, disease, and the ravages of poverty and war. I've seen more tragedy in my years with Project C.U.R.E. than anyone should ever see in a lifetime.

In the 1990s, I spent a lot of time in Russia and the old Soviet Federation as the culture and economy were unraveling after the collapse of the Soviet system. I was there when the citizens of Ukraine stormed the poorly guarded armories and took weapons for their own protection. I learned that practically anyone could purchase military weapons as long as he or she had the right contacts and the correct amount of money. I also discovered that no one knows where all those rockets, bombs, missiles, and warheads have ended up, since no one was really watching over the stockpile of Soviet weaponry.

So, yes, I'm aware of the mess this old world is in. In fact, there's a very real possibility that in the next thirty seconds, a massive solar flare or an EMP (electromagnetic pulse) attack from a nuclear warhead could jolt us back into the Dark Ages, destroying our electrical grid and wreaking havoc with utility services, food storage and delivery, medical services, information and communication systems, transportation, and government services.

An EMP attack would render useless anything with an electronic circuit or chip. Everything from a simple car part to the pacemaker that keeps your heart pumping to the complicated infrastructure running the world's financial systems to the gadgets, appliances, and other items three hundred million Americans rely on for daily life would likely be knocked out in seconds.[1] Now that's a mess.

No one has a free hall pass or an exemption certificate tucked away to escape a disaster scenario should it unfold. And yet as Walt Disney used to say, "I always like to look on the optimistic side of life, but I am realistic enough to know that life is a complex matter."

Curbside Choices: Vice or Virtue

Earlier we toyed with the idea that each of us is standing on the curbside at the intersection of culture and economics holding our own market baskets, which are filled with our most valuable possessions. How we allocate the contents of our baskets can have a tremendous impact on the world around us—for better or for worse. As we stand there at the curbside, a continual flow of traffic passes through the intersection in front of us. That intersection is where transformation takes place. We're not passive observers of what happens there; we're active participants. The possessions we choose to take from our market baskets and inject into the action unfolding at the intersection will alter the course of history in one way or another.

So each of us is confronted with a crucial question: "What'cha gonna do with what'cha got?" We can't dodge the question or ignore it, because like it or not, change happens, and each of us is an agent of change.

As you gaze into your market basket, you find all kinds of financial, personal, relational, spiritual, and special possessions. From those contents, what would you say is the most strategic and important possession you could inject into the flow of traffic? In a very real sense, you face a proverbial fork-in-the-road decision as you consider what to do with the possessions at your disposal.

Since the dawn of time, people have used the contents of their market baskets for good or for evil. History has demonstrated repeatedly that humans have a remarkable capacity for evil. Evil can be observed in the lawless, corrupt, and greedy actions of government leaders, corporate executives, homegrown community thugs, and even fraudulent social-services recipients. Murderous despots like Hitler, Stalin, Mussolini, Pol Pot, Saddam Hussein, and Idi Amin may spring to mind when we think of evil. But we are *all* capable of using the contents of our market baskets for selfish and evil purposes.

Most of us are familiar with the Seven Deadly Sins, or vices, but let's review them briefly as we think about the choices and opportunities that confront us at the intersection of economics and culture:

1. *Lust*—an inordinate and intense desire to fulfill cravings for sex, power, fame, money, and even food
2. *Gluttony*—excessive and wanton indulgence to the point of obscene waste
3. *Greed*—a selfish and rapacious desire for material things in contrast to eternal values, as well as a violation of the value, rights, or dignity of others.
4. *Sloth*—physical or spiritual laziness, complacency, or apathy

5. *Wrath or rage*—uncontrolled hatred or anger often expressed through violence and revenge

6. *Envy*—insatiable desire to be better and have more than others, whether material things, abilities, status, recognition, or rewards

7. *Pride*—puffed up with self-importance and an entitlement mentality; the belief that one is better than others

Have you noticed that these deadly vices are fueled by an obsession with self? When self is king, our capacity for evil knows no limits.

What can we do when such a powerful capacity for selfishness and evil exists in the world? As my old grandfather used to tell me "Don't let evil beat you up, but beat up and overcome evil with *good*."

Thankfully history has demonstrated that humans also have a remarkable capacity for *virtue*. We can *choose* to be the dispensers of kindness, charity, forbearance, justice, righteousness, and benevolence in a hurting world. It's an amazing thing to see the goodness of people who use their God-given abilities to make this world a better place.

Virtue is a tremendously powerful force that can overcome vice and its destructive impact. Simply put, *virtue* is "moral excellence [goodness]" or "integrity of character."[2] Virtue is said to be the key building block not only of a successful and happy life but of a successful civilization. Without virtue, a culture self-destructs.

Vices come naturally in our fallen human condition, but virtues are often quite difficult to develop. As the poet Alexander Pope famously said, "To err is human; to forgive, divine." Mr. Pope got it right. If we want to develop supernatural qualities, we can't rely on natural human effort. Virtue can only be attained through supernatural empowerment.

In the fifth century, the Christian poet Aurelius Clemens Prudentius compiled one of the most enduring contrastive lists of vices and virtues in his allegorical poem "Psychomachia" ("The Contest of the Soul"). The seven heavenly virtues, as they were called, were widely acclaimed throughout Europe during the Middle Ages, and many people believed that practicing them offered protection from being ensnared in the Seven Deadly Sins. With that time-tested list in mind, let's investigate these heavenly virtues:

1. *Chastity.* Chastity involves purity in thought and behavior, as well as a morally wholesome character. In modern times, chastity has been viewed as a prudish attitude toward sexuality, but that couldn't be further from the truth. Chastity embraces sexuality as God intended it to be and demonstrates respect not only for oneself but for others by striving to be self-controlled and pure minded. A chaste person not only abstains from inordinate or improper sexual conduct but embraces a healthy lifestyle and seeks to avoid temptation and corruption.

2. *Temperance.* Like chastity, temperance is often considered antiquated in today's vernacular, and yet it's an essential virtue in a world where restraint and self-control are becoming increasingly rare qualities. Temperance in modern times has typically referred to moderation in consuming alcohol, but temperate people practice moderation in all things, especially with respect to indulging their natural appetites and passions.

3. *Charity.* Considered the moral building block of major world religions, charity or love is expressed in benevolent attitudes and actions toward others without expecting something in return. Charity is often expressed in acts of generosity toward people in need. Generosity and self-sacrifice, even toward our enemies, are indeed at the heart of love. In an age where self-interest prevails, showing true charity toward everyone we meet is like shining a beacon in the darkness. People today are desperate for real love, not just platitudes. Charity is the most powerful force for good in this world.

4. *Diligence.* This virtue refers to being steadfast, persistent, and zealous in accomplishing a task. Diligence requires patient endurance and strives for excellence even when no one is watching. Diligent people believe that anything worth doing is worth doing well, and they guard against carelessness, apathy, mediocrity, and laziness. Diligence is sorely needed in a fast-food culture where people demand immediate gratification and have little patience for tasks that require persistence and attention to detail.

5. *Patience*. A patient person these days is a precious gift. Patience refers to a willingness to resolve injustices and conflicts peacefully instead of resorting to strife or violence. Akin to patience is *forbearance*, which literally means "to bear with." When we exhibit patience, we're demonstrating a willingness to bear with others in spite of irritation, delay, provocation, or misfortune. We choose to show restraint and kindness instead of reacting in a show of temper, irritation, or complaint.

6. *Kindness*. Kindness is a spirit of magnanimity combined with compassion and cheerfulness. Kind people express thoughtful consideration and empathy toward others, maintaining a friendly demeanor regardless of how others treat them. True kindness acts without prejudice, resentment, or ill will toward its recipients. Many people are superficially nice, but their friendliness evaporates when it isn't reciprocated. Kindness, however, remains magnanimous and compassionate in all circumstances.

7. *Humility*. Saint Augustine observed that "humility is the foundation of all other virtues. … If you plan to build a tall house of virtues, you must first lay deep foundations of humility." Humility is everything that pride is not. It is a frank and modest estimate or opinion of one's own importance, rank, or position, which, at the same time, confers on others the respect, honor, and value their positions deserve. A humble spirit also correctly perceives its value in relation to God and the world he created. Humility is often confused with low self-esteem or a doormat mentality, but true humility is a character strength, not a weakness. Humble people are so secure in their identity that they don't need to prove themselves to anyone. They walk through life with quiet confidence and strength.

Virtue outshines vice any day of the week, wouldn't you say?

So getting back to the question I asked earlier: What is the most strategic and important possession you could take from your market basket and inject into the flow of traffic? In my opinion, *virtue* is the one possession that can make the greatest impact at the intersection of culture and economics. If each of us concentrated our efforts on developing virtue in our lives, we'd do this old world a great deal of good and give evil a swift kick in the pants.

As you stand on the curbside with your market basket, remember that you have the power to influence the direction, timing, and outcome of events in the world by injecting goodness into the flow of traffic.

An Asian friend of mine once shared with me this thought-provoking proverb:

Past the seeker as he prayed came the crippled and the beggar and the beaten.
And seeing them, the holy one went down into deep prayer and cried out,
"Great God, how is it that a loving Creator can see such things and yet do nothing
about them?"
And out of a long silence, God said, "I did do something. I made you."

The Virtue of Ebenezer Scrooge

We can learn a great deal about virtue from a character by the name of Ebenezer Scrooge. How is that possible, you ask? Well, if you've read the Charles Dickens classic *A Christmas Carol*,[3] you know how the story ends. But first things first. As we raise the curtain on old Scrooge early in the story, we find that his business partner, Marley, has died. The spirit of Marley suddenly returns from the grave to visit greedy old Scrooge and warn him to mend his ways before it's too late.

Scrooge hears Marley coming down the hallway dragging the chains he forged "link by link" throughout his life. Terrified, Scrooge double-locks his door, but Marley's spirit glides into the bedroom with ease.

"Speak comfort to me, Jacob!" Scrooge pleads after hearing Marley's opening monologue of gloom and doom.

But the spirit replies, "I have none to give. … No space of regret can make amends for one life's opportunity misused!"

When Scrooge assures Marley that he was a "good man of business," the spirit wails, "Business! Mankind was my business. The common welfare was my business; charity, mercy, forbearance, and benevolence, were all my business. The dealings of my trade were but a drop of water in the comprehensive ocean of my business!"

Then Marley delivers a deathblow: "I am here tonight to warn you: that you have yet a chance and hope of escaping my fate."

Scrooge, this "squeezing, wrenching, grasping, scraping, clutching, covetous old sinner" is shaken to the core—this man who is "hard and sharp as flint [and] solitary as an oyster"; indeed, whose only friend is Bob Cratchit, his abused, underpaid clerk.

But the nightmare has just begun for Scrooge. The spirits of the past, the present, and the future follow behind Marley in succession to show Scrooge what has been, what is, and what will be. They literally scare the hell out of old Scrooge, and finally he cries out, "I am not the man I was. I will not be the man I must have been. … I will honour Christmas in my heart, and try to keep it all the year. … I will not shut out the lessons [the spirits] teach."

As the curtain closes on Scrooge's life, we see a bitter, greedy, unsociable scoundrel transformed into a man of virtue:

> Scrooge was better than his word. He did it all, and infinitely more: and to
> Tiny Tim who did not die, he was a second father. He became as good a
> friend, as good a master, and as good a man as the good old city knew, or any
> other good old city, town, or borough in the good old world. Some people
> laughed to see the alteration in him, but he let them laugh and little heeded
> them. … His own heart laughed and that was quite enough for him.[4]

In the end, Scrooge decides to inject some good old-fashioned virtue into the intersection of culture and economics. Instead of the usual contents of greed, selfishness, pride, and wrath, he draws out of his market basket the virtues of charity, humility, and kindness. His investment in virtue pays remarkable dividends of goodness that change his entire world, as well as the lives of Tiny Tim, Bob Cratchit, and hundreds of others.

I wonder what would happen if we injected some goodness from our individual market baskets into the flow of traffic. As we help others at the curbside become better off, we might discover some rich inner rewards.

THE ECONOMICS
OF THE INTERIOR

At this point, we've talked quite a bit about economic and cultural systems, market baskets, vices and virtues, and the changes that take place at the intersection of culture and economics. We've also discussed how our choices as individuals influence what happens at that intersection. The contents we remove from our market baskets and inject into the flow of traffic can change the course of history forever. But will our actions ultimately make the world better off?

The answer to that question revolves around a concept I like to call *the economics of the interior*. Of all the choices we make in life, the most important decision is which system we will embrace and rely on to direct our thoughts and guide our actions in every area of life.

An Internal Navigational System

Whether we realize it or not, each of us is guided by an internal economic system that is, in a very real sense, a navigational system that's custom designed for individuals. Like any navigational system, it conveys essential information and coordinates that help us determine the direction our lives are headed and make the necessary corrections if we drift off course.

The *economics of the interior* refers to a set of economic, cultural, and spiritual truths (or principles) that direct our thoughts, motives, values, beliefs, and actions. It's very much like an internal, invisible mechanism that guides our decisions and behaviors. External systems may pressure us to conform to principles and practices we don't agree with, but the economics of the interior always reflects our true convictions.

No matter which system we choose to embrace, that system, with its values and principles, is assimilated into the core of our being—body, spirit, and soul, including our minds, our wills, and our emotions. The economics of the interior influences and impacts everything we do at the curbside and every choice we make about the possessions we inject into the flow of traffic. This is why our choice of systems is so critical. As I've said before, systems matter.

If our inner compass is geared toward greed and other human vices, our choices, and ultimately our lives, will reflect those priorities. The economics of the interior in such a case may benefit our personal interests but won't make others better off.

All my years of traveling around this old world have taught me that no man-made system can replicate the divine system of goodness, integrity, and love. If we embrace this divine system and assimilate it into the economics of the interior, love and goodness will dominate our choices and direct us toward pursuits that will benefit others and influence the course of history.

As you stand on the curbside at the intersection of culture and economics, you have a number of choices to make:

- How will you use the contents of your market basket—your financial, personal, relational, spiritual, and special possessions?
- How will you manage all of the resources, capacities, liabilities, and opportunities that are unique to your situation?
- How will you deal with the external economic systems that pressure you to conform to their particular values and principles?
- How can you make good decisions about the resources and capacities you inject into the flow of traffic to influence the course of history so that you and others will become better off?

All of these decisions ultimately boil down to the simple question, "What'cha gonna do with what'cha got?"

One Tough and Compassionate Lady

When it comes to personifying the economics of the interior, I don't believe there is any finer example in our contemporary era than Baroness Caroline Cox.

Caroline Cox became a registered nurse in the 1950s and met her future husband, Murray, while working at a London hospital. After marrying and starting a family, Caroline earned a first-class honors degree in sociology at the University of London and a master's degree in economics. She went on to write several books on nursing and teach sociology at a London university, where she collided head-on with academic elites who forced their Marxist views on the students.

After enduring years of their intimidation, she coauthored *The Rape of Reason*, which courageously exposed their warped beliefs at a time when standing for democratic ideals was extremely unpopular. In 1977, Caroline embraced a new challenge as the director of nursing education research at Chelsea College, University of London.

Prime minister Margaret Thatcher was so impressed with Caroline's indomitable spirit, high energy, and brilliant work that she exerted her considerable influence to see Caroline become Baroness Cox of Queensbury and a life peer in the House of Lords in January of 1983. Lady Cox became Deputy Speaker of the House of Lords in 1985 and served in that position until 2005.

What did Baroness Caroline Cox do with her new title and position of influence?

Instead of just parking herself on the red leather benches in the gilded chamber of the House of Lords, Baroness Cox began using the precious assets in her market basket to help other people become better off. Penetrating the Iron Curtain of the Soviet Union, she risked her life to deliver load after load of desperately needed humanitarian goods to Communist Poland, Romania, and Armenia.

Lady Cox also sought to help the people of Nagorno-Karabakh. Mass murderer

Joseph Stalin had arbitrarily separated the small country from its motherland, Armenia, and had given it to Azerbaijan to placate the violent Muslim extremists. Eventually Azerbaijan, Turkey, and Russia embarked on a plan of ethnic cleansing that would systematically annihilate the inhabitants of Nagorno-Karabakh. Baroness Cox stood up in the House of Lords and brought the situation to the attention of Parliament and the world. No one else seemed to care … except Baroness Caroline Cox. But Lady Cox didn't just talk about the situation; she sprang into action. She traveled to Yerevan, Armenia, climbed into a military helicopter, and flew into the war-torn enclave of Nagorno-Karabakh to help evacuate the wounded and dying. Her nurse's training also equipped her to provide essential medical care to the evacuees.

I first met Baroness Cox in 1997 when she and her executive assistant, Stuart Windsor, came to Colorado to get better acquainted with Project C.U.R.E. After learning about our international experience, they had determined that we were the best organization to help them with their humanitarian work in Nagorno-Karabakh.

I joined the baroness on her thirty-ninth trip to the decimated country, where I learned that she had once walked directly through the line of weapon fire, waving a white tablecloth attached to a branch, and crossed the Azerbaijan border to personally confront the Muslim thugs who had been murdering the Karabakh inhabitants and torching their homes. She was determined to meet these thugs face-to-face so they would take her seriously. They soon learned that Caroline Cox was one tough lady.

Over the years her compassionate endeavors have led her into many zones of conflict throughout the world, including Sudan, Nigeria, Uganda, Myanmar (Burma), and Indonesia. She even injected goodness into the former Soviet Federation, helping government officials change their policies on orphaned and abandoned children and establish a foster-care system that would place children in families rather than institutions. (I would enthusiastically encourage you to read Andrew Boyd's book *Baroness Cox: A Voice for the Voiceless*, which chronicles Lady Cox's inspiring life story and the magnificent humanitarian work she has been involved in).

Baroness Cox has received many international awards for her humanitarian work, including the Commander's Cross of the Order of Merit of the Republic of Poland; the prestigious Wilberforce Award; the international Mother Teresa Award; the Mkhitar Gosh medal conferred by the president of the Republic of Armenia; the anniversary medal presented by Lech Walesa, former president of Poland; and an honorary fellowship of the Royal College of Physicians in London, England.

After all these years, Lady Caroline Cox is still investing her life, her unique abilities, and her influential position to spread goodness around the globe. She's a classic example of how just one person, guided by the economics of the interior, can help others become better off.

Snapshots of Goodness

Throughout history, countless individuals like Baroness Caroline Cox have become agents of change in the world. Guided by the economics of the interior, they used the contents of their market baskets to help others become better off. Whether the impact of their actions created a giant tsunami of change or just a tiny ripple, all of these folks had one quality in common: goodness. Allow me to share a few of their stories.

Mother Teresa

Macedonian-born native Agnes Bojaxhiu, known throughout the world as Mother Teresa, became a Catholic nun at the age of eighteen and was eventually sent to Calcutta, India, to teach at a girls' high school. In 1946, she experienced a second calling—a "call within a call"—and devoted the latter half of her life to caring for the poorest of the poor in Calcutta. Her order, the Missionaries of Charity, not only cared for the sick, disabled, and dying but established mobile health clinics, a nursing home and orphanage, and a leper colony. In spite of deep struggles with her faith, she never wavered in her commitment to helping those in need.

Daniel Kalnin

Daniel escaped from Burma in 1965 at the age of eighteen, determined to get an education and return to his country someday to help his people. He eventually made his way to the United States, where he met his wife and attended Bible college. After graduating, he and his wife became missionaries in Thailand, but Daniel was prohibited from returning to Burma. He had been separated from his birth family for nearly forty years, and he longed to return to his native land.

While in Thailand, Daniel founded the Barefoot Doctors project, which enabled individuals from remote villages in Burma to come to Thailand for basic first-aid training. In many cases, the people in these villages had no access to any kind of medical care. Some of the trainees had to walk for weeks from remote areas and cross illegally into Thailand. The barefoot doctors received one month of training for three years in a row and returned to their villages equipped to provide basic emergency medical care for their people. When Daniel was finally able to visit Burma in 2001, the people were overwhelmed to meet the man who had loved them enough to send help back to his native country.

Muhammad Yunus

Known as the "banker to the poor," Yunus received the Nobel Peace Prize in 2006 for his work with the Grameen Bank, which provides affordable loans and financial training to the poor so they can establish their own business endeavors.[1] Yunus began providing small loans from his personal assets to poor basket weavers in Bangladesh in the 1970s. His vision to eliminate poverty through microlending gradually expanded in subsequent years, and the Grameen Bank was launched. His microlending model has been replicated in more than one hundred other countries, offering hope and help to economically disadvantaged people around the world.

Gene Osborne

My friend Gene is a successful entrepreneur. When Gene was in his early teens, he figured out a way to buy a big truck, and soon he built a trucking business into a successful enterprise. Then somewhere along the line, he switched to developing real estate and became successful at that entrepreneurial endeavor as well.

One day a Project C.U.R.E. board member brought Gene to our Denver warehouse for a tour. At lunch Gene said he liked what he saw and bluntly asked, "Okay, Jackson, what do you need most today?"

I looked at him and replied, "I need two big-box trucks with hydraulic liftgates on the back to move heavy equipment and medical goods to our warehouse. Right now, I'm embarrassed to say, I'm not being a very good steward, because I'm paying good money to rent two trucks when we should own them free and clear."

Gene then asked me to write down exactly what I needed. When I handed him the paper, he put it in his pocket and told me that I would have my trucks the following week. "By the way," he said, "how do you want them painted?"

But Gene didn't stop there. He not only helped us buy our own Project C.U.R.E. warehouse in Brighton, Colorado, but he also invited us to move our international headquarters into his large office building, free of rent and utility payments. Then he went to Nashville, Tennessee, with us and helped us buy a beautiful warehouse on a ten-acre piece of land with expansive views of the medical community. He was also instrumental in helping us get into our present warehouse site in Centennial, Colorado.

Gene and his lovely wife, Lyn, recently purchased books about Project C.U.R.E. to be handed out as gifts to all of our wonderful volunteers so they can learn as much about Project C.U.R.E. as possible. Guided by the economics of goodness and generosity, Gene and Lyn understand the economic principles that made America great, and they have invested their lives in helping other people become better off.

Project C.U.R.E. Volunteers and Staff

How could I talk about people guided by the economics of the interior without recognizing the heroes who have helped to make Project C.U.R.E. the largest and most effective distributor of donated medical goods in the world today? It takes a whole *lot* of people to run our operations, including our massive warehouses in five states and a dozen collection centers around the United States. Since Project

C.U.R.E. donates medical supplies and equipment to recipients in more than 130 countries, we rely almost entirely on volunteers—including me—to handle our operations. Presently we have more than seventeen thousand volunteers, and none of these folks receive a salary.

The scope of volunteer involvement at Project C.U.R.E. is amazingly diverse. Certified and licensed volunteers drive Project C.U.R.E. trucks to collect donated medical goods from manufacturers, suppliers, hospitals, and large clinics. And our CURE Couriers regularly drive their own vehicles to pick up donated goods from local clinics, distributors, and retail outlets. Thousands of individuals from service groups, churches, civic organizations, universities, and corporations gather at Project C.U.R.E. facilities to sort medical goods, pack boxes, label and bar-code items, and palletize and properly stack the material that is ready to ship. Others professionally organize and operate the warehouse system. Still others learn the art of packing medical goods in forty-foot oceangoing cargo containers. Each year, hundreds more volunteers travel overseas with Project C.U.R.E. to perform needs assessments and conduct medical clinics. It isn't unusual for some of our volunteers to give of their time regularly for twelve or more years to help others end up better off.

Most of these precious volunteers never meet any of the people they have unselfishly helped. Recipients of the donated medical goods don't come all the way to American to say, "Thank you for saving my life," or "Thanks for making it possible for my wife to have surgery." Such miracles happen, but our faithful volunteers may never hear the words of thanks. Yet they volunteer anyway, because their internal navigational systems assure them that they're doing the right thing with their lives. They have decided to give the best of their lives for the rest of their lives to help make others better off. In my book that makes them heroes.

The Reset Button: A Personal Decision

Whenever I tell people that Anna Marie and I gave away our accumulated wealth and decided to spend the best of our lives for the rest of our lives making other people better off, they sometimes ask, "So, Dr. Jackson, how did that relinquishment thing work out for you? Did you have to file for bankruptcy, or did God reward you financially for being such a good guy and giving away millions?"

The simple answer to that is neither. Anna Marie and I didn't give away our wealth to get something in return. We simply gave it away because that was what we felt we ought to do. It was a personal decision. As we examined the economics of the interior that had been guiding our lives and informing our choices, we realized that we needed to push the reset button and get our priorities straightened out.

I've often pondered the strange and glorious adventure Anna Marie and I embarked on when we decided to stake our very lives on God's call to relinquish our earthly wealth and pursue goodness. We had worked hard our entire lives and had acquired sixteen times more wealth than I thought we would ever have in our entire lifetime. But it wasn't satisfying. We were doing well, but we weren't happy. I needed a radical transformation that would shift the entire paradigm of my life. I had to change from being a person bent on *getting* to being a person bent on *giving*.

Our new adventure required Anna Marie and me to intentionally let go of those things we considered our security blankets but were, in fact, chains of bondage. We then had to develop a new expectation and trust in God as our security. We had to walk to the edge of the cliff and then over the edge, trusting that God would catch us or teach us how to fly.

Guided by a new economics of the interior, Anna Marie and I purposely chose to take our hands off the earthly things that will last only for a short time so that we could lay hold of the abundant things that will last forever. We discovered that true abundance is possible only through relinquishment. In the process of relinquishing our accumulated wealth, we learned to joyfully let go of our own expectations about what we *thought* we needed and trust that God, in his preeminent wisdom, would supply what we *truly* needed. He did just that … and so much more. As a result, Anna Marie and I began using the contents of our market baskets to make others better off. Through Project C.U.R.E. and billions of dollars' worth of donated medical supplies and equipment, we saw the impact of goodness in saving tens of thousands of lives around the world.

We never suggest that others should follow suit and give away all of their accumulated wealth, but pushing the reset button and embracing the economics of goodness was the best business deal I've ever made.

MAKING OTHERS
BETTER OFF

In my boyhood home, my dad used to tell his three high-energy, entrepreneurial boys, "Take what you have and make it into what you want or need. And always make sure that *everyone* ends up better off."

The idea of "better off" is arguably a bit slippery. In some ways it's quite objective. Let's say you swallow a piece of food in a restaurant and suddenly start choking. You're objectively better off if I happen to be sitting next to you and am proficient at administering the Heimlich maneuver. I squeeze you and dislodge the blockage, and you don't die on the spot. Everyone in the restaurant would agree that you are now better off.

But better off can also be subjective. You may define the term based upon your personal perceptions and attitudes. Your definition of what *better off* means may differ from everyone else's. The same is true of words like *fortunate, beneficial, propitious*, or *worthwhile*. What these words mean to one person may mean something totally different to another.

Rather than getting hung up on the subjective or objective nature of the term, let's stick with a more generalized definition. *Better off* means "a transition into a more advantageous position in life."

When my brothers and I were in business together as adults, we noticed an interesting phenomenon: our efforts were successful when those around us—our customers, our workers, our suppliers, and our families—ended up better off. If our business efforts were failing, we would inevitably discover that we ourselves were failing to make other people better off somewhere down the line. We might have structured a very smart and lucrative deal only to find the whole thing beginning to unravel a few days later. That's when we would meet at the local coffee shop and make a list of everyone involved in the deal. We'd put ourselves in the shoes of the key players and ask ourselves if each one perceived that he was coming out of the deal better off. Once we figured out the kinks in the deal, we went back and ironed them out. When we ensured that everyone would end up better off, the deal would come together and stay together.

The Secret of Success

The principle I've just outlined is true for everyone who participates in a free-enterprise system. We succeed only to the extent that we make other people better off. When we're free to pursue what we feel is best for us individually, we create wealth, but we also run the risk of failing. Failure forces us to go back to the drawing board and figure out what went wrong. More often than not, we discover that our original plan didn't make other people better off, and we need to make some course corrections. When we're successful in our endeavors to make others better off, we're rewarded commensurately and get to keep our reward, which motivates us to repeat the experience.

During the 1960s and 1970s, our Jackson Brothers Investment company amassed tremendous wealth helping other people solve their problems. Our primary goal was to ensure that other people became better off. We not only succeeded in accomplishing that goal, but we became wealthier as a side benefit.

Anna Marie and I established Project C.U.R.E. with that same goal in mind: we wanted everyone involved in the endeavor to become better off. Many international humanitarian nonprofit organizations fail because they abuse or neglect one or more parties in the deal. But Project C.U.R.E. has tried to stay mindful of the needs of all the parties involved as we collect and distribute donated medical goods to more than 130 countries around the world.

Obviously, the poor and sick people who are the ultimate recipients of these medical goods need to end up better off. But the donors must also feel they are better off for giving to meet various needs. Project partners, like the Rotary Club, international businesses, and religious organizations must come out of the endeavor better off as well. Our Project C.U.R.E. volunteers here in America must also end up better off as they invest countless hours ensuring that the medical supplies and equipment are collected, inventoried, packed, and shipped to their destinations. And the various government entities and staff people involved—foreign and domestic—need to perceive an advantage to facilitating the endeavor. Unless every one of these groups and individuals ends up better off, Project C.U.R.E. will fail to achieve its goal.

Thankfully Project C.U.R.E. has been extremely successful at making people better off. In fact, we've become the largest handler of donated medical goods in the world. We've also received the GuideStar Exchange Silver Seal and the Charity Navigator four-star rating, and Forbes ranked Project C.U.R.E. as one of the twenty most efficient large US charities.

When you and I use the contents of our market baskets to help meet the needs of others, we discover the joy and satisfaction of injecting goodness into people's lives and making a positive difference. As a result, we find ourselves wanting more of these kinds of experiences.

In a world where instant gratification is king, making people better off quickly becomes a lifelong venture that yields amazing rewards for everyone.

"Everyone Can Help Someone"

Helping others become better off may sound like a great idea, but perhaps you're wondering, *What can I do? I don't even know where to begin.*

When we look at the mess the world is in and the desperate need that surrounds us, it can feel overwhelming. We can be tempted to throw up our hands in despair and conclude that whatever we might try to do can't possibly be enough. Even in our own communities, the need seems so massive and the resources so limited. But that's a mind-set of scarcity, not abundance.

To put things in perspective and lay the groundwork for a plan of action, let me share another important principle I learned while working with Project C.U.R.E. in the Ukraine following the collapse of the Soviet Union. As I was performing needs assessments at various clinics and hospitals in Lviv and Ternopil, the director of a large hospital told me that many Ukrainians wanted to escape the horrific conditions in Ukraine and live in America. But not this man. Even though he had been offered a lucrative position in the United States, he decided to remain in Ukraine and dedicate his life to rebuilding his country's devastated health-care system.

"I can't help everybody," he said, "but I can make a difference."

On another occasion, I accompanied my Ukrainian friend Meeche to a local prison hospital, where I had been asked to perform a needs assessment. On the way, we picked up bread and sugar at the state-run grocery store, and Meeche brought along a large knife to cut the loaves. He just grinned when I asked, "Are you really crazy enough to think you can take that knife into the prison with us?"

Inside the stone prison, surrounded by razor wire and armed guards, Meeche took out his knife and cut each loaf of bread into quarters; then we followed the guards into the main building carrying our boxes containing bread and sugar, little bags of candy, and Ukrainian Bibles. When we entered the hospital wards, the stench threatened to gag me. Each ward was secured by solid steel doors with bars and locks, and there was only one small, tightly sealed window high up on a wall. The most severely ill patients were kept in large open wards farther down the corridor, and at the very end were the advanced-cancer wards. All of these patients were prisoners who had been confined to the hospital wards. Their illnesses had become their death sentences. The old Soviet prison system was inhumane, but medical care in the prisons was nightmarish. I'll never erase the images of suffering I witnessed that day.

Into this nightmare Meeche and his friends regularly brought a little food and candy and words of hope from the Bible in the Ukrainian language. Meeche told me, "No one else cares for these lost souls, but we can help make our beloved Ukraine a better place by taking love to them."

During my visit to Ukraine, I witnessed terrible suffering and overwhelming need, but something president Ronald Reagan said helped me through those insanely difficult days: "We can't help everyone, but everyone can help someone."

He was right. We may not be able to make a huge difference or help everyone, but we can make a small difference in the life of one person. And if each of us makes an effort, however small, to help others become better off, we'll end up making a big difference together.

Colonel Vi's Army

We can't undo the mistakes of the past, but we can push the reset button and determine that we will spend the best of our lives for the rest of our lives making others better off. A former Vietnamese colonel did just that.

When Anna Marie and I visited the city of Tam Ky, Vietnam, in 2004, we received a special invitation to meet Colonel Thuong Tuong Vi at the Mercy Center for the Performing Arts. I had assumed that the colonel was a man until I heard someone refer to Madame Vi.

Madame Vi's background was quite intriguing and mysterious. She was a full colonel in the Vietnamese army, a former member of the Central Committee of the People's Army, and a high-profile member of the Hanoi cultural society. As a professional singer and dancer, she was also one of Vietnam's most renowned artistic performers and received countless awards, especially for entertaining the military and the People's Army.

When Madame Vi became a devout Christian, the radical change in her life intrigued the Communist Party elite. Her comrades watched with interest as she gathered disadvantaged children from the streets and brought them to her Mercy Centers.

"I no longer wanted fame and attention," Madame Vi told me. "I only had a burning desire to help other people, especially young, disadvantaged children."

The center in Tam Ky housed 72 children, and she also provided housing for 120 children in Da Nang and 180 orphans in Hanoi. In addition to housing, Madame Vi trained the children in the performing arts.

When Anna Marie and I met Madame Vi at the center in Tam Ky, she graciously ushered us into a conference room, where we got acquainted. Madame Vi shared with us her dream of having Project C.U.R.E. establish and equip a small medical clinic for the children in each of her centers. "I want to provide the best for my children, because one day they will be our new leaders. I want them to see and feel what is possible."

Madame Vi then escorted us upstairs to a small performing theater. After we were seated, she leaned over and whispered, "God showed me that one day I will no longer have my talents and my beautiful voice, and I should take those talents now and transfer them into orphans, homeless children, and crippled children who otherwise would have no hope of a good future."

At that point, a handsome young Vietnamese boy stepped forward on the stage and welcomed us in flawless English. Then the children entertained us with traditional Vietnam folk songs, performed beautifully with graceful choreography and hand signing. As the concert continued, I looked around in amazement. There wasn't a smidgeon of doubt that the famed performer had poured her life and talents into the former street urchins. The meticulously trained, young singers communicated with warm smiles, sparkling eye contact, vibrant body language, and stage presence. The harmonies were incredible, and each word was sung in phonetically perfect English.

The concert ended with two familiar Christmas carols and the song "He's Got the Whole World in His Hand." There wasn't a dry eye in the room.

After the performance, I promised Madame Vi that Project C.U.R.E. would help her set up and equip the medical clinics at her centers. I also asked her what her People's Army friends thought about her selection of songs.

"I teach the underprivileged children diversity of culture and perfect English," she said. "The party officials love it. I first teach the children to sing the songs phonetically, and while learning the lyrics, they begin to ask questions about what the songwriter was saying. I simply answer all their questions so that they can sing the songs with understanding and feeling. Strangely enough, they all fall in love with my friend Jesus."

Then Colonel Thuong Tuong Vi confided to me, "I can't go back and start a new beginning, but I can start today and make a new ending."

Investing the best of our lives for the rest of our lives to make other people better off pays lasting dividends. The goodness that results from such efforts ripples through nations and societies, impacting untold numbers of hurting and needy people. We may never have the opportunity to meet any of these people, but the waves of goodness that lap against distant shores will return to wash over us as well, healing us and meeting our own needs.

CONCLUSION

BETTER OFF FOR AMERICA

In 2008, the State Department and the Department of Defense designated me to represent the United States at a weeklong international strategic planning conference in Africa. Over the course of the week, I became well acquainted with the other conference participants and particularly enjoyed getting to know an articulate gentleman from Europe. This man just happened to be the head of a well-known international humanitarian organization funded primarily by American endowments.

On the fourth day of the conference, we discussed the role of America in providing humanitarian aid to Africa over the years. At that moment, my new friend gave a little speech that made my jaw drop to my tie. It went something like this:

> Americans are just going to have to learn to adjust to living with ten-dollar-a-gallon gasoline prices and higher prices for everything. They have it too good! America ended up with all the wealth, and the rest of the world has ended up in poverty. Americans must now divide their wealth with the rest of the world, or the disparity and inequality will get worse.
>
> We must realize that those people who are involved in humanitarian work have a product to sell to the American people. They are so rich and spoiled and so guilty of opulence that it is absolutely mandatory for them to purge that guilt in some way to make themselves feel better. Their psyches are so screwed up that they'll pay a high price to get rid of their guilt by championing humanitarian causes in places like Africa. We've been given the job to help the Americans feel better about themselves and their greed.

Many Americans agree with my European friend that by some twist of fate, the United States ended up with all the wealth, and the rest of the world has been deprived of their slice of the pie. They have concluded that greed and an entitlement mentality are largely to blame for making America better off than everyone else. Consumed with guilt, they have bought into a zero-sum mentality, believing that redistribution of wealth is the only way to make amends. Sadly, they haven't the slightest inkling why America ended up so much better off than the rest of the world.

What they fail to understand is that the American people have been blessed not because of some arbitrary twist of fate or some greedy endeavor to deprive the rest of the world of its meager slice of pie, but because the participants in the American experiment of 1776 honored the rule of law, valued freedom of choice, and understood from hard experience the need for limited government.

These American patriots often spoke of God's kindness and generosity and thanked him for his blessings. They not only respected the rights of individuals to own personal property and pursue their own interests, but they were careful not to confuse self-interest with greed or selfishness. They discovered that the more generously they gave to help their neighbors become better off, the better off they became as individuals. Their morality, honesty, industriousness, and religious faith bonded them together as a community and gave them the strength to overcome the hardships and uncertainties they faced as a new nation.

The economics of the interior guided these men, and when they injected their market-basket contents into the flow of traffic, they transformed the world. The wealth of America resided not only in its material resources but in the good and generous *character* of its people, who reached out to help others become better off.

Had the founders not played their individual roles and made their unique contributions at that particular moment in history, the great American experiment would never have come to pass, and the possibility of freedom, goodness, and abundance might still be just an unfulfilled dream.

We Become What We Believe

My dad believed that people become what they think about all day long. So did King Solomon and Maxwell Maltz. Solomon put it this way: "As [a man] thinks in his heart, so is he" (Proverbs 23:7, NKJV). In America's case, beliefs became a nation. Beliefs originate in the interior economic systems of individuals and ultimately expand to families, communities, and nations. Those beliefs will continue in perpetuity unless or until an entirely new paradigm overrides them. That's the way the system works.

The nation that was born in 1776 was the product of the personal beliefs of those who participated in the great experiment. But without the revolutionary principles of the Magna Carta and the groundbreaking discoveries of Adam Smith, it's quite possible that America would still be just a vision in the minds of the oppressed masses.

No other nation in the history of humanity has been as generous as America. If there were such a thing as *gross national generosity* (GNG), America would outshine every other country in the world. Typically, the US government will give out of our nation's wealth nearly fifty billion dollars in aid to other less fortunate countries. That's a lot of money. No other nation in history even comes close to that amount. In addition, private US donors, including ministries and churches, businesses, foundations, nonprofit groups like Project C.U.R.E., and individual Americans give tens of billions of dollars each year in charitable contributions to help needy people around the world.

What would this old world look like without the kindness and generosity of America?

All that goodness began in the hearts and minds of America's founders, and our freedom was forged by the fiery events of 1776. As a direct result of that generation's sacrifices, Americans in subsequent generations prospered—and so did the world. However, America has no guarantee of enduring as the crafters of the 1776 experiment envisioned it. On October 11, 1798, John Adams, the second president of the United States, declared to the officers of the Massachusetts militia,

> We have no government armed with power capable of contending with human passions unbridled by morality and religion. Avarice, ambition, revenge, or gallantry, would break the strongest cords of our Constitution as a whale goes through a net. Our Constitution was made only for a moral and religious people. It is wholly inadequate to the government of any other.[1]

Looking across our nation today, we can see the great American experiment and its blessings fading into the mists of time as our government whittles away our precious freedoms. Individual choice is eroding as more and more of us become dependent on government to take care of us. Excessive taxation and government regulations have stymied our inherent incentive to create and produce. Our religious and cultural heritage is being uprooted before our very eyes. The personal rights and freedoms guaranteed us in the Constitution are vanishing, and the Constitution itself is being trampled on. Justice, impartiality, and the rule of law are becoming extinct.

Alexis de Tocqueville reportedly observed that "a [republic] will continue to exist up until the time that voters discover that they can vote themselves generous gifts from the public treasury." That indeed is the situation we find ourselves in today. Stuck in a pit of greed and entitlement, many Americans have bought into the lie that it isn't necessary to work for a living if they can vote for a living. The more dependent Americans become on government handouts, the harder it will be to relinquish that easy money in favor of liberty and abundance.

But all is not lost. The great American experiment need not be declared dead. The men and women who dedicated their lives and "sacred honor" to make America a land of freedom and opportunity need not have toiled, sacrificed, or died in vain. We can still reclaim the rich heritage of 1776 and pass it on to future generations.

At the Crossroads

To the folks who wistfully comment that they wish we could return to the way things used to be, when our nation was truly great and good, I heartily respond, "We *can* restore the American dream of becoming better off … if we have the courage and resolve to make the *right* course corrections."

Anyone who has ever tried to bake a cake without using the right ingredients soon discovers that the end result is nothing like the intended product. And more often than not, the results are disastrous. In the pages of this book, we've explored the essential ingredients that made America better off and investigated an economic system that is designed to benefit everyone. As we stand at the intersection of culture and economics, each of us must now decide what we will do with that information. Never before in the history of our nation have systems mattered more.

The final chapter in the intriguing drama of America has not yet been written, but we are standing at an existential crossroads. The life-and-death message the old prophet Jeremiah proclaimed to the people of Israel is vitally relevant today:

> Stand at the crossroads and look;
> > ask for the ancient paths,
> ask where the good way is, and walk in it,
> > and you will find rest for your souls. (Jeremiah 6:16)

Voices from America's past are calling us to retrace our steps to the bedrock values of liberty, goodness, and abundance that the founders fought so sacrificially to secure for us. The issue boils down to a single question: Will we continue clinging to a system of scarcity, selfish entitlement, and phony redistribution, or will we break free from that impoverished paradigm and return to the only system in the history of the world that has ever led to abundance?

I've been engaged in a little supposin' once again. Instead of spreading other people's money around until it runs out and we end up in the poorhouse, suppose we dedicate our lives to spreading liberty and goodness around so that everyone ends up better off.

NOTES

CHAPTER 1

1. *The World Factbook 2013–2014* (Washington, DC: Central Intelligence Agency, 2013), statistics for January 1, 2014, cited in Index Mundi, accessed July 14, 2015, http://www.indexmundi.com/g/r.aspx?c=zi&v=67.

2. Table 25, "OTC Foreign Exchange Turnover by Currency in April 1995–2013," in *Triennial Central Bank Survey: Global and Foreign Exchange Market Turnover in 2013* (Basel, Switzerland: Bank for International Settlements, 2014), 72, http://www.bis .org/publ/rpfxf13fxt.pdf.

3. Mark Yeandle, *The Global Financial Centres Index 16* (London: Z/Yen Group, 2014), 2, http://www.longfinance.net/images/GFCI16_22September2014.pdf.

4. Data updated for 2015, "People and Society," in *The World Factbook 2013–2014* (Washington, DC: Central Intelligence Agency, 2014), https://www.cia.gov/library /publications/the-world-factbook/geos/hk.html.

5. Heritage Foundation, "2015 Index of Economic Freedom: Hong Kong," accessed July 14, 2015, http://www.heritage.org/index/country/hongkong.

6. Hong Kong, per-capita income, January 1, 2014, cited in Index Mundi, accessed July 14, 2015, http://www.indexmundi.com/g/r.aspx?c=zi&v=67.

CHAPTER 2

1. Jude Wanniski, *The Way the World Works* (New York: Regnery, 1998), 180.

2. Ibid., 181.

3. Will Durant, *The Story of Civilization*, vol. 2, *The Life of Greece* (New York: Simon and Schuster, 1966), 552.

4. Ibid., *Caesar and Christ*, 3:182–83.

5. Ibid., 182.

6. Ibid., 177.

7. Ibid., 192.

8. Kingsley B. Smellie, *Great Britain Since 1688: A Modern History* (Ann Arbor: University of Michigan Press, 1962), 139.

9. Ibid., 140.

10. Declaration of Independence, July 4, 1776.

CHAPTER 3

1. Declaration of Independence, July 4, 1776.

2. Patrick Henry, "Liberty or Death" speech, Second Virginia Convention, Richmond, Virginia, March 23, 1775, http://www.patrickhenrycenter.com/Speeches .aspx#LIBERTY.

3. Declaration of Independence.

4. Ibid.

5. Benson John Lossing, *Biographical Sketches of the Signers of the Declaration of Independence* (New York: George F. Cooledge and Brother, 1848), 73.

6. Ibid., 89.

7. Ibid., 80.

8. Ibid., 226.

9. Ibid., 204.

10. Ibid., 192.

11. John Adams, quote from John Adams Historical Society, accessed January 13, 2016, http://www.john-adams-heritage.com/quotes/.

12. Preamble of the US Constitution, September 17, 1787.

13. Abraham Lincoln, Gettysburg Address, November 19, 1863.

CHAPTER 5

1. Muhammad Yunus, "Grameen Bank at a Glance," Grameen Bank, September 2005, http://www.grameen-info.org/grameen-bank-at-a-glance/.

CHAPTER 6

1. David Hume, *Hume Political Essays*, ed. Knud Haakonssen (Cambridge, UK: Cambridge University Press, 1994), 62.

2. Greg Toppo, "China Baby Policy Too Little, Too Late," *USA Today*, October 30–November 1, 2015.

3. Laura Fitzpatrick, "China's One-Child Policy," *Time*, July 27, 2009, http://content .time.com/time/world/article/0,8599,1912861,00.html.

4. Ibid.

CHAPTER 7

1. David Hume, *Hume Political Essays*, ed. Knud Haakonssen (Cambridge, UK: Cambridge University Press, 1994), 115.
2. Adam Smith, "Of the Origin and Use of Money," in *An Inquiry into the Nature and Causes of the Wealth of Nations* (1776), public domain, Gutenberg e-book, released February 28, 2009, http://www.gutenberg.org/files/3300/3300-h/3300-h.htm#link2HCH0004.
3. Franklin D. Roosevelt, quoted in Gerhard Peters and John T. Woolley, "Executive Order 6102—Requiring Gold Coin, Gold Bullion, and Gold Certificates to Be Delivered to the Government," April 5, 1933, American Presidency Project, accessed January 16, 2016, http://www.presidency.ucsb.edu/ws/index.php?pid=14611.
4. "Table C-92—US Reserve Assets, 1946–72," in *Economic Report of the President: Transmitted to the Congress January 1973* (Washington, DC: Government Printing Office, 1973), 299, http://www.presidency.ucsb.edu/economic_reports/1973.pdf.
5. *Encyclopedia Britannica Online*, s.v. "credit card," accessed June 3, 2015, http://www.britannica.com/EBchecked/topic/142321/credit-card.

CHAPTER 10

1. "Consumer Price Index," Bureau of Labor Statistics, accessed July 16, 2015, http://www.bls.gov/cpi/.
2. Adam Smith, "Of the Origin and Use of Money," in *An Inquiry into the Nature and Causes of the Wealth of Nations*, (1776), public domain, Gutenberg e-book, released February 28, 2009, http://www.gutenberg.org/files/3300/3300-h/3300-h.htm#link2HCH0004.
3. John Maynard Keynes, *The Economic Consequences of the Peace* (New York: Harcourt Brace Jovanovich, 1920), 236.

CHAPTER 11

1. Campbell R. McConnell and Stanley L. Brue, *Economics: Principles, Problems, and Policies*, 17th ed. (New York: McGraw-Hill/Irwin, 2008), 263.

2. "US Business Cycle Expansions and Contractions," National Bureau of Economic Research, September 20, 2010, http://www.nber.org/cycles.html.

3. John R. Walter, "Depression-Era Bank Failures: The Great Contagion or the Great Shakeout?" *Economic Quarterly* 91, no. 1 (Winter 2005): 39, http://www.unc.edu /~salemi/Econ423/Depression_Era_Bank_Failures.pdf.

4. Information from multiple sources, including *Encyclopedia Britannica Online*, s.v. "Great Depression," http://www.britannica.com/EBchecked/topic/243118 /Great-Depression; and Milton Friedman, *Free to Choose* (New York: Harcourt Brace Jovanovich, 1980).

CHAPTER 12

1. Bureau of Labor Statistics Household Survey, December 2015, cited in "Economic News Release: Employment Situation Summary," Bureau of Labor Statistics, January 8, 2016, http://www.bls.gov/news.release/empsit.nr0.htm; see also "US Unemployment," Department of Numbers, accessed January 14, 2016, http://www .deptofnumbers.com/unemployment/us/.

2. High-tax states in 2015, "States with the Highest and Lowest Taxes," TurboTax, accessed January 14, 2016, https://turbotax.intuit.com/tax-tools/tax-tips /Taxes-101/States-with-the-Highest-and-Lowest-Taxes/INF23232.html.

3. Ibid.

CHAPTER 13

1. John Maynard Keynes, *The Economic Consequences of the Peace* (New York: Harcourt Brace Jovanovich, 1920), 236.

2. See Elizabeth Spiers, "The Great Inflation Cover-up," *Fortune*, April 3, 2008, http://archive.fortune.com/2008/03/31/magazines/fortune/spiers_cpi.fortune /index.htm.

3. Board of Governors of the Federal Reserve System, press release, January 25, 2012, http://www.federalreserve.gov/newsevents/press/monetary/20120 125c.htm.

4. "Current FAQs: Why Does the Federal Reserve Aim for 2 Percent Inflation over Time?" Board of Governors of the Federal Reserve System, updated January 26, 2015, http://www.federalreserve.gov/faqs/economy_14400.htm.

CHAPTER 14

1. John Woolley and Gerhard Peters, "Election of 1932," American Presidency Project, accessed January 14, 2016, http://www.presidency.ucsb.edu/showelection .php?year=1932.

2. Franklin D. Roosevelt, "Commonwealth Club Address," San Francisco, California, September 23, 1932, transcript, Heritage Foundation, "FDR's Commonwealth Club Address," accessed January 15, 2016, http://www.heritage.org/initiatives /first-principles/primary-sources/fdrs-commonwealth-club-address.

3. Franklin D. Roosevelt, quoted in Gerhard Peters and John T. Woolley, "Inaugural Address," March 4, 1933, American Presidency Project, accessed January 15, 2016, http://www.presidency.ucsb.edu/ws/index.php?pid=14473.

4. Franklin D. Roosevelt, cited in Gerhard Peters and John T. Woolley, "Proclamation 2039—Declaring Bank Holiday," March 6, 1933, American Presidency Project, accessed January 15, 2016, http://www.presidency.ucsb.edu/ws/?pid=14661.

5. Franklin D. Roosevelt, "Inaugural Address," March 4, 1933.

6. Merlo J. Pusey, "FDR vs. the Supreme Court," *American Heritage* 9, no. 3 (April 1958).

7. John Maynard Keynes, "An Open Letter to President Roosevelt," *New York Times*, December 31, 1933; see also "New Deal Documents," New Deal Network, accessed July 15, 2015, http://newdeal.feri.org/misc/keynes2.htm.

8. Letter from John Maynard Keynes to Franklin D. Roosevelt, King's College, Cambridge, England, February 1, 1938, Franklin D. Roosevelt Presidential Library and Museum, accessed January 15, 2016, http://www.fdrlibrary.marist.edu/aboutfdr /pdfs/smFDR-Keynes_1938.pdf.

9. Sudeep Reddy, "The New Old Big Thing in Economics: J. M. Keynes," *Wall Street Journal*, January 8, 2009, http://www.wsj.com/articles/SB123137373330762769.

CHAPTER 15

1. Declaration of Independence, July 4, 1776.

2. Max Lerner, in Adam Smith, *An Inquiry into the Nature and Causes of the Wealth of Nations* (New York: Random House, 1937), vii.

3. Adam Smith, "Of the Origin and Use of Money," in *An Inquiry into the Nature and Causes of the Wealth of Nations*, public domain, Gutenberg e-book, February 28, 2009, http://www.gutenberg.org/files/3300/3300-h/3300-h.htm#link2HCH0004.

4. Ibid.

5. Ibid.

6. Ibid.

7. Ibid.

8. Karl Marx, *The Communist Manifesto*, ed. Friedrich Engels (UK: Harriman House, 1848), 1828.

9. Karl Marx, "Critique of the Gotha Programme: Marginal Notes to the Programme of the German Workers' Party," letter to Wilhelm Bracke, May 5, 1875, http://www .archive.org/stream/CritiqueOfTheGothaProgramme/cgp_djvu.txt.

10. Ibid.

11. Delos B. McKown, *The Classical Marxist Critiques of Religion: Marx, Engels, Lenin, Kautsky* (The Hague: Martinus Nijhoff, 1975), 10, 12.

12. Vladimir Ilyich Lenin, *Essential Works of Lenin: "What Is to Be Done?" and Other Writings*, ed. Henry M. Christman (New York: Bantam Books, 1966; Dover Publications, 1987), e-book, 150.

CHAPTER 16

1. Karl Marx, "Critique of the Gotha Programme: Marginal Notes to the Programme of the German Workers' Party," letter to Wilhelm Bracke, May 5, 1875, http://www .archive.org/stream/CritiqueOfTheGothaProgramme/cgp_djvu.txt.

2. *Doctor Zhivago*, directed by David Lean (Beverly Hills, CA: Metro-Goldwyn-Mayer, 1965).

CHAPTER 17

1. Adam Smith, *An Inquiry into the Nature and Causes of the Wealth of Nations*, public domain, Gutenberg e-book, February 28, 2009, http://www.gutenberg .org/files/3300/3300-h/3300-h.htm#link2HCH0004.

2. Ibid.

3. Ibid.

4. Milton Friedman and Rose Friedman, *Free to Choose: A Personal Statement* (New York: Harcourt, 1980), 14.

5. Adam Smith, "Of the Origin and Use of Money," in *An Inquiry into the Nature and Causes of the Wealth of Nations*.

6. Ibid.

7. Ibid.

CHAPTER 18

1. Adam Smith, "Of the Origin and Use of Money," in *An Inquiry into the Nature and Causes of the Wealth of Nations*, public domain, Gutenberg e-book, February 28, 2009, http://www.gutenberg.org/files/3300/3300-h/3300-h.htm#link2HCH0004.

2. Ibid.

3. Ibid.

CHAPTER 19

1. Data from National Institute of Food and Agriculture, United States Department of Agriculture, cited in "Historical Timeline—Farmers and the Land," Growing a Nation: The Story of American Agriculture, accessed January 15, 2016, http://www.ag classroom.org/gan/timeline/farmers_land.htm.

2. Letter from J. B. Lee to congressman Ed Foreman, March 20, 1963, in *Congressional Record*, vol. 109, 1364, quoted in Andrew Carroll, ed., *Letters of a Nation: A Collection of Extraordinary American Letters* (New York: Broadway Books, 1999), 262–63.See also http://www.mocavo.com/Congressional-Record-Volume-109-2/551629/1364.

3. "The History of SNAP," SNAP to Health!, accessed July 18, 2015, http://www.snap tohealth.org/snap/the-history-of-snap/.

4. Chris Halsne and Chris Koeberl, "Welfare Cash Pulled from ATMs Inside Colorado Pot Shops," Fox31 Denver, February 19, 2014, accessed January 15, 2016, http://kdvr.com/2014/02/19/welfare-cash-pulled-from-atms-inside-colorado-pot-shops/.

5. US Department of Agriculture, "Supplemental Nutrition Assistance Program (SNAP): A Short History of SNAP," November 20, 2014, http://www.fns.usda.gov/snap/short-history-snap.

6. US Department of Agriculture, "Supplemental Nutrition Assistance Program (SNAP)," Benefits.gov, accessed July 18, 2015, http://www.benefits.gov/benefits/benefit-details/361.

7. "SNAP: Frequently Asked Questions," SNAP to Health!, accessed January 15, 2016, http://www.snaptohealth.org/snap/snap-frequently-asked-questions/#howmany.

8. National School Lunch Act, Pub. L. No. 396, 79th Cong., June 4, 1946, 60 Stat. 231, quoted in Gordon W. Gunderson, "National School Lunch Act," USDA Food and Nutrition Service, June 17, 2014, http://www.fns.usda.gov/nslp/history_5.

9. See Campbell R. McConnell, Stanley L. Brue, and Sean Flynn, *Economics: Principles, Problems, and Policies*, 17th ed. (Boston: McGraw-Hill, 2008), 599–605.

10. Dwight D. Eisenhower, statement at White House signing ceremony, July 10, 1954, in *Public Papers of the Presidents of the United States: Dwight D. Eisenhower* (Washington, DC: Government Printing Office, 1960), 626; see also Gerhard Peters and John T. Woolley, "162—Statement by the President upon Signing the Agricultural Trade Development and Assistance Act of 1954," July 10, 1954, American Presidency Project, http://www.presidency.ucsb.edu/ws/index.php?pid=24605 &st=&st1=.

11. John F. Kennedy, quoted in Gerhard Peters and John T. Woolley, "Remarks of Senator John F. Kennedy, Corn Palace, Mitchell, SD," September 22, 1960, American Presidency Project, http://www.presidency.ucsb.edu/ws/index.php?pid=74154.

12. Data from National Institute of Food and Agriculture, USDA, cited in "Historical Timeline—Farmers and the Land," http://www.agclassroom.org/gan/timeline /farmers_land.htm.

13. Earl Butz, quoted in Mary Link, "Candidates Clash in Farmbelt," *Cedar Rapids Gazette*, September 29, 1976.

14. Earl Butz, quoted in Heather H. Scholar, "Federal Farm Policies Hit," *Reading Eagle*, October 23, 1973.

CHAPTER 20

1. C. S. Lewis, letter to Mrs. Hook, December 29, 1958, in C. S. Lewis *Letters of C. S. Lewis*, ed. W. H. Lewis (Orlando, FL: Harcourt, 1988), 475–76.

2. Elsie E. Egermeier, *Boy's Stories of Great Men* (Anderson, IN: Gospel Trumpet Company,1931), 182-91.

3. Maxwell Maltz, *Psycho-Cybernetics: A New Way to Get More Living out of Life* (New York: Simon and Schuster, 1960), chaps. 2 and 3.

4. International Energy Agency, "Selected Indicators for 2013," in *Key World Energy Statistics* (Paris: International Energy Agency, 2015), 48, http://www.iea.org /publications/freepublications/publication/KeyWorld_Statistics_2015.pdf.

5. *Encyclopedia Britannica*, s.v. "George Washington Carver"; see also Raleigh H. Merritt, *From Captivity to Fame, or the Life of George Washington Carver* (Boston: Meador Publishing, 1929).

CHAPTER 21

1. Dwight D. Eisenhower, quoted in Gerhard Peters and John T. Woolley, "256—Address Before the General Assembly of the United Nations on Peaceful Uses of Atomic Energy, New York City," December 8, 1953, American Presidency Project, accessed January 16, 2016, http://www.presidency.ucsb.edu/ws/index.php?pid =9774&st=&st1=.

2. Eric Schmidt, from keynote speech, Abu Dhabi Media Summit, Abu Dhabi, March 12, 2010.

3. "Moore's Law, or How Overall Processing Power for Computers Will Double Every Two Years," accessed January 8, 2016, http://www.mooreslaw.org/; see also Gordon E. Moore, "Cramming More Components onto Integrated circuits," *Electronics*, April 19, 1965, 114–17, http://www.cs.utexas.edu/~fussell/courses/cs352h/papers /moore.pdf.

4. Stephen Shankland, "IBM Chips: Let There Be Light Signals," CNET.com, December 1, 2010, http://www.cnet.com/news/ibm-chips-let-there-be-light-signals/#!.

5. Kevin Ashton, "That 'Internet of Things' Thing," *RFID Journal*, July 22, 2009, http://www.rfidjournal.com/articles/view?4986.

6. FTC Staff Report, "Executive Summary," in *Internet of Things: Privacy and Security in a Connected World* (Washington, DC: Federal Trade Commission, 2015), i, https://www.ftc.gov/system/files/documents/reports/federal-trade-commission -staff-report-november-2013-workshop-entitled-internet-things-privacy/150127 iotrpt.pdf.

7. Ibid.

8. Vint Cerf, quoted in Peter H. Diamandis and Steven Kotler, "The Abundance Builders," *Futurist* 46, no. 4 (July–August 2012), http://www.wfs.org/futurist/july -august-2012-vol-46-no-4/abundance-builders.

9. Maury Harris, in Rob Wile, "North Dakota Oil Production Just Set New Record," *Business Insider*, December 20, 2012, http://www.businessinsider.com.au /december-north-dakota-oil-production-2012-12.

10. Statistics from North Dakota Department of Mineral Resources, cited in Tessa Berenson, "Oil Is the New Gold: Inside North Dakota's Oil Rush," *Time*, June 24, 2014, http://time.com/2911836/oil-north-dakota/.

11. Bureau of Labor Statistics, "Economy at a Glance: North Dakota," July 7, 2015, http://www.bls.gov/eag/eag.nd.htm; Bureau of Labor Statistics, "Labor Force Statistics from the Current Population Survey: Unemployment Rate," July 8, 2015, http://data.bls.gov/timeseries/LNS14000000.

12. "Williston, ND, Unemployment Rate Report," Homefacts.com, accessed July 8, 2015, http://www.homefacts.com/unemployment/North-Dakota/Williams-County/Williston.html.

13. Ed Yardeni, quoted in Rob Wile, "There's a Huge Bullish Story on Energy and the Economy, and It's Sitting Right Below the Radar," *Business Insider*, January 8, 2014, http://www.businessinsider.com/us-energy-boom-continues-to-surprise-2014-1.

14. Ibid.

15. "Oil Glut to Persist in 2016 as Global Growth Demand Slows—IEA," Reuters, October 13, 2015, http://www.reuters.com/article/oil-iea-idUSL9N0O802G20151013; see also US Energy Information Administration, *Annual Energy Outlook 2015* (Washington, DC: Government Printing Office, 2015), http://www.eia.gov/forecasts/aeo/pdf/0383(2015).pdf.

16. US Energy Information Administration, "Executive Summary," in *Annual Energy Outlook 2015*, http://www.eia.gov/forecasts/aeo/executive_summary.cfm.

17. Christopher Helman, "ExxonMobil: Green Company of the Year," *Forbes*, August 6, 2009, http://www.forbes.com/forbes/2009/0824/energy-oil-exxonmobil-green-company-of-year.html.

18. Logan Ward et al., "Craig Venter Thinks He Can Change the World: He Already Has," *Popular Mechanics*, October 4, 2010, http://www.popularmechanics.com/science/health/a6197/craig-venter-profile/.

19. Von Philip Bethge, "Oozing Biofuel: Algae Could Solve World's Fuel Crisis, ABC News, July 31, 2011, http://abcnews.go.com/International/algae-solve-worlds-fuel-crisis/story?id=14181088&singlePage=true.

20. Kevin Bullis, "Exxon Takes Algae Fuel Back to the Drawing Board," *MIT Technology Review*, May 20, 2013, http://www.technologyreview.com/view/515041/exxon-takes-algae-fuel-back-to-the-drawing-board/.

21. Information on Slingshot in Susan L. Nasr, "How the Slingshot Water Purifier Works," HowStuffWorks.com, July 27, 2009, http://science.howstuffworks.com/environmental /green-tech/remediation/slingshot-water-purifier.htm; see also Ryan Bergeron, "Segway Inventor Takes Aim at Thirst with Slingshot," CNN.com, September 11, 2009, http://www.cnn.com/2009/TECH/09/11/kamen.water.slingshot/index.html.

22. Shane Hickey, "A Tsunami and No Water to Drink: How Disaster Inspired Lifesaving Invention," *Guardian*, June 1, 2014, http://www.theguardian.com/global -development/2014/jun/01/how-disaster-inspired-lifesaving-water-filtration -invention.

23. Ibid.

24. Michael Pritchard, "How to Make Filthy Water Drinkable," transcript, TED.com, August 2009, http://www.ted.com/talks/michael_pritchard_invents_a_water_filter /transcript.

25. "IBM Makes Water Clean with Smarter, More Energy-Efficient Purification," news release, IBM, March 16, 2009, http://www-03.ibm.com/press/us/en/pressrelease /26921.wss.

26. Environmental Protection Agency, "Leaks Can Run, but They Can't Hide," Water Sense, accessed July 8, 2015, http://www.epa.gov/watersense/our_water/fix_a _leak.html.

27. Matylda Czarnecka, "Bill and Melinda Gates Foundation Grants $1.5M to Turn Human Waste into Biofuel," TechCrunch.com, June 17, 2011, http://techcrunch. com/2011/06/17/bill-and-melinda-gates-foundation-grants-1-5m-to-turn-human -waste-into-biofuel/ .

28. Bill and Melinda Gates Foundation, "Water, Sanitation, and Hygiene: Reinvent the Toilet Challenge," Fact Sheet, 2013, https://docs.gatesfoundation.org/Documents /Fact_Sheet_Reinvent_the_Toilet_Challenge.pdf.

29. Ibid.

30. Chris Weller, "Bill Gates Is Backing This Waterless Toilet That Could Revolutionize Global Sanitation," *Business Insider*, January 12, 2016, http://www.businessinsider. com/the-waterless-toilet-that-could-save-global-sanitation-2016-1.

31. Gates Foundation, "Water, Sanitation, and Hygiene," accessed January 12, 2016, https://docs.gatesfoundation.org/Documents/Fact_Sheet_Reinvent_the_Toilet _Challenge.pdf.

32. Bill and Melinda Gates Foundation, "Reinvent the Toilet Challenge: Strategy Overview," accessed July 8, 2015, http://www.gatesfoundation.org/What-We-Do/Global-Development/Reinvent-the-Toilet-Challenge.

CHAPTER 22

1. Stephanie Crawford, "How 3-D Printing Works," How Stuff Works Tech, accessed January 16, 2016, http://computer.howstuffworks.com/3-d-printing1.htm.

2. Tony Hoffman, "3D Printing: What You Need to Know," *PC Magazine*, January 4, 2016, http://www.pcmag.com/article2/0,2817,2394720,00.asp.

3. Carl Bass, "The Past, Present, and Future of 3-D Printing," *Washington Post*, August 24, 2011, https://www.washingtonpost.com/national/on-innovations/the-past-present-and-future-of-3-d-printing/2011/08/21/gIQAg4fJZJ_story.html.

4. Hoffman, "3D Printing," http://www.pcmag.com/article2/0,2817,2394720,00.asp.

5. Ibid.

6. "Doctors Use 3-D Printing to Remove, Reimplant Skull of Toddler with Rare Condition," FoxNews.com, July 21, 2015, http://www.foxnews.com/health/2015/07/21/doctors-use-3-d-printing-to-remove-re-implant-skull-toddler-with-rare-condition/?intcmp=ob_homepage_health&intcmp=obnetwork.

7. Joseph Flaherty, "This Dress Is Made from 3-D Printed Plastic, but Flows Like Fabric," *Wired*, December 9, 2014, http://www.wired.com/2014/12/dress-made-3-d-printed-plastic-flows-like-fabric/; see also Anatol Locker, "3D Printed Fashion: Designer Printed Her Entire Collection at Home," All3DP.com, July 25, 2015, https://all3dp.com/3d-printed-fashion-danit-peleg-printed-her-collection-at-home/.

8. Jenny C. Aker and Isaac M. Mbiti, "Mobile Phones and Economic Development in Africa," *Journal of Economic Perspectives* 24, no. 3 (Summer 2010): 210, http://pubs.aeaweb.org/doi/pdfplus/10.1257/jep.24.3.207.

9. Data from International Telecommunication Union, May 2014, cited in "Global Mobile Statistics 2014," MobiForge, May 16, 2014, https://mobiforge.com/research-analysis/global-mobile-statistics-2014-part-a-mobile-subscribers-handset-market-share-mobile-operators#subscribers.

10. Patrik Cerwal, ed., *Ericsson Mobility Report on the Pulse of the Networked Society* (Stockholm, Sweden: Ericsson, 2015), 4, 7, http://www.ericsson.com/res/docs/2015/ericsson-mobility-report-june-2015.pdf.

11. "About Nathan Myhrvold," TerraPower, accessed July 8, 2015, http://terrapower
    .com/people/nathan-myhrvold.

12. Information regarding the benefits of TerraPower and the traveling wave reactor
    (TWR), including cost, safety, environmental protection, and other factors, can be
    found at http://terrapower.com/pages/benefits.

13. Dr. Nathan Myrhvold, quoted in "TerraPower Joins Other Big Ideas in 'Abundance,'"
    Intellectual Ventures, February 21, 2012, accessed July 8, 2015, http://www
    .intellectualventures.com/insights/archives/terrapower-joins-other-big-ideas
    -in-abundance.

14. David Szondy, "Small Modular Nuclear Reactors—the Future of Energy?" *Gizmag*,
    accessed July 8, 2015, http://www.gizmag.com/small-modular-nuclear-reactors
    /20860/.

15. Ibid.

16. Will Ferguson, "First 'Small Modular' Nuclear Reactors Planned for Tennessee,"
    National Geographic, June 7, 2013, http://news.nationalgeographic.com/news
    /energy/2013/06/130605-small-modular-nuclear-reactors-tennessee/.

CHAPTER 23

1. John S. Foster Jr. et al., *Report of the Commission to Assess the Threat to the United
   States from Electromagnetic Pulse (EMP) Attack: Critical National Infrastructures*
   (Washington, DC: Government Printing Office, 2008).

2. *Merriam-Webster Unabridged*, s.v. "virtue."

3. Quotes in this section from Charles Dickens, *A Christmas Carol* (Wheaton, IL:
   Tyndale, 1997), 4, 16–19, 82.

4. Ibid., 93.

CHAPTER 24

1. "Muhammad Yunus—Biographical," Nobelprize.org, accessed January 16, 2016,
   http://www.nobelprize.org/nobel_prizes/peace/laureates/2006/yunus-bio.html.

CONCLUSION

1. John Adams, quoted in Charles Francis Adams, *The Works of John Adams, Second
   President of the United States* (Boston: Little, Brown, 1854), 9:229.